A Memoir

Louise James

First published by Ultimate World Publishing 2021
Copyright © 2021 Louise James

ISBN

Paperback: 978-1-922828-58-3
Ebook: 978-1-922497-69-7

Louise James has asserted her rights under the Copyright, Designs and Patents Act 1988 to be identified as the author of this work. The information in this book is based on the author's experiences and opinions. The publisher specifically disclaims responsibility for any adverse consequences which may result from use of the information contained herein. Permission to use information has been sought by the author. Any breaches will be rectified in further editions of the book.

All rights reserved. No part of this publication may be reproduced, stored in or introduced into a retrieval system, or transmitted in any form, or by any means (electronic, mechanical, photocopying, recording or otherwise) without the prior written permission of the author. Any person who does any unauthorised act in relation to this publication may be liable to criminal prosecution and civil claims for damages. Enquiries should be made through the publisher.

Cover design: Ultimate World Publishing / Andy Toohey
Layout and typesetting: Ultimate World Publishing
Editors: Rebecca Low, Marinda Wilkinson

Ultimate World Publishing
Diamond Creek,
Victoria Australia 3089
www.writeabook.com.au

Dedication

For my children

Thank you for walking beside me,
inspiring me and being with me at the finishing line.

I love you both today, tomorrow and forever x

&

For all those who have walked this path before me,
those who may no longer be here to hold their children and
loved ones, and to those who are embarking on this journey.

I wish you strength, hope and happiness
to live a full and free life.

A life with **no full stops.**

What People Are Saying About
No Full Stops

'*No Full Stops* is a refreshing reflection on living with cancer through the emotional, humorous and very real accounts of one woman's experience. Louise has gifted readers with the ability to sit in the skin of a cancer patient and understand a little of what the experience and pain may be like, but her quirky and magnetic personality ensures a light, enjoyable and funny read.'

Kirstine Lumb-McKay,
Writer & Award-winning Journalist

'A very honest account written from the heart. Louise taps into the gravity of cancer but also the surprising moments of humour and joy which can coexist during such adversity.

Sharing commonly unspoken insights, *No Full Stops* chronicles a year defined by cancer diagnosis and treatment, interspersed with more lighthearted anecdotes, resulting in an informative, candid and relatable story about life, cancer, family, and the depths of human resilience. It also captures insightfully the post cancer journey, where a different kind of personal struggle emerges. The reader can't help but reflect on how they might integrate similar experience and make meaning from a "second chance" at life.

As the main cancer story unfolds against the daily grind of family routines, vet appointments, school lunches and numerous cups of tea, we are reminded of the importance these seemingly benign routines provide to give structure, rhythm and pockets of certainty during a crisis.

'I'd commend *No Full Stops* as a comforting companion for those facing their own diagnosis, treatment and recovery journey and equally helpful to friends and families trying to understand their loved one's perspective. A valuable read if you're reflecting on the impact of cancer or any other life altering event.'

**Dr Rebecca Jackson,
PhD, Psychologist & Author of *The Journey of You***

Contents

Foreword		ix
1.	Good Intentions	1
2.	Cup of Tea?	13
3.	Needlepoint	23
4.	Facebook Official	29
5.	To Be or Not to Be Cancer?	35
6.	In Black and White	49
7.	Keeping Up Appearances	53
8.	The Cavalry Arrives	59
9.	Game of Knives	65
10.	The Will to Live	73
11.	50 Shades of Chemo	81
12.	Treatment Treadmill	91
13.	Cause and Effect	113
14.	All Things Bald and Beautiful	121
15.	Cancer, Models Own	129
16.	Radioactive, Radioactive	139
17.	The Aftermath	151
18.	There's No Womb at the Inn	159
19.	Stops and Starts	171
20.	Five Years Later	185
Afterword		191
Acknowledgements		195
About the Author		199

Foreword

I've always charged through life, moving from one event to another at a frantic pace. Those who know me, will tell you how I talk with breathless speed as if full stops are a luxury and not required. That was, until March 2015, when an unexpected diagnosis of breast cancer almost became a full stop to my life's script.

I initially resented the challenge this presented, as I felt I had already fulfilled my quota of life's trials and tribulations. I had fought an uphill battle to finalise the details of my son's diagnosis of Asperger's syndrome, was navigating the choppy waters of co-parenting, faced financial hardship and made the decision to relocate the family to the countryside. As a single mother of two, I felt overwhelmed with this unplanned diversion.

Cancer, like a pebble once thrown into the water, has a far-reaching ripple effect. Although you are rarely alone during the journey, there are times that you may *feel* alone at sea and barely treading water.

I don't profess this book is a 101 of cancer basics or a 'how to do' cancer. In the years since I was diagnosed, many of the treatment options have changed, and research and published evidence continues to evolve. This is my story of a roller-coaster year of operations, treatments and the lessons learnt along the way. A dash of humour, a loose armor of resilience and the love and support from family, friends and strangers, helped pulled me through.

Here, I share with you a medley of memories and the intimate aspects of my cancer journey—the light, the dark, and sometimes, the inappropriate. I hope that by sharing my story, those going through similar challenges might not feel so isolated. I also trust it provides an insight for family, friends and carers on what to expect. Ultimately, I hope that through this experience, we all come out richer for it and know that ***it's never too late to rewrite your storyline.***

May you find something here to help you **connect, heal,** and **grow.**

Disclaimer

This is my story. For both legal and moral reasons, in some instances, dates, locations, names and other identifiers have been changed. In some cases, where consent has been provided, real names have been used. Any references to medical information relate to my specific and unique diagnosis and treatment pathway, pertinent at the time. In telling my story, I am cognisant that I only write from my perspective and memories. I do not presume to tell the story of others who are featured prominently in this book.

If this book triggers painful memories and/or unusual reactions, please seek medical and professional help and support.

My wish, above anything else, is that it will provide you with some insight, hope and laughter too.

Cup of tea?

With just those three short words,
my world would come to a **Full Stop.**

Everything was about to change.
Nothing would ever be the same again.

1

Good Intentions

I started 2015 with gusto. I decided to join CrossFit. Well, when I say 'I', it was more of a group decision. I was just excited to be getting out of the house to spend time with friends. I had no clue what I was actually signing up for. I'm a dive in for the fun of it and ask questions later kind of girl. Little did I realise that the CrossFit style of fitness is more extreme boot camp for army cadets. My usual vibe is classes where you only move when the instructor is directly looking at you. My head told me, 'go hard or go home' to get my fitness back on track. In this case, I should have just stayed home.

I hadn't even opened my front door to head out for the first session when I dropped my metal water bottle on my big toe. It left an impressive bruise. I should have taken that as a sign and turned back, but I pressed on. It would only be a week-long program, so how hard could it be? After all, in 1998, I had managed to complete a four-day trek to Machu Picchu with no training. This should be a walk in the park.

After the first session, I found myself walking around the house like a newly saddled drover. When going to the bathroom, I had to hold on to the sides of the walls and gently lower myself to meet the toilet seat. I have a high pain threshold, but my muscles began to tremble and strain under this new regime. Those five days felt like I had completed an assault course with Bear Grylls. Somehow, I made it. I was exhausted, but I made it. I held on to the completion certificate with pride. I even laminated it. Take that, you doubters. I would like to say my goal was to have a killer body, but really, it was for more practical reasons.

Just a few years earlier in 2012, we had moved from a flat in Bondi to a house in the Southern Highlands. That is, my two children, Mr Mac (then aged eight), Miss Lipstick (then aged six) and an ever-neurotic chocolate Labrador puppy called Coco. It had been a hard few years leading up to the move, having separated from the children's father four years earlier.

Our relationship began as a whirlwind of love and excitement for a future together. I had been told I would struggle to get pregnant with endometriosis, so we were thrilled when we found out I was pregnant. We started making plans for our future family.

Endometriosis had been my evil puppet master for many years. I was a late starter and had my first period at sixteen. There were some concerns that my skeletal frame at the time was the cause, but no further investigations were made. I was so relieved and grateful to reach womanhood that I wore my pain like a badge of honour. My pain levels gradually became unbearable. I plucked up the courage to request their eviction. The doctor at boarding school was an older gentleman and not the easiest to broker conversations with. I was handed a script for the contraception pill at seventeen, told to take it every day with no breaks between packets and sent on my way. I didn't think to question it. I just did as I was told. I was good at that.

Over the years, my pelvic pain became more prominent. It wasn't until I was thirty that I sought help. I was staying with my sister in South Africa at the time, on the cusp of a daring solo adventure around Asia. The pain crescendoed. I began to have visions of being airlifted out of Vietnam. I was afraid of being alone in a foreign country left to discuss my lady parts. Equipped with comprehensive travel insurance for my upcoming trip to cover any medical fees, I sprang into action.

I booked an appointment to see the next available gynaecologist—another male doctor. It was the first time I had ever heard the word 'endometriosis'. I played an Oscar-winning performance of a dutiful and unquestioning patient. I agreed to have day surgery the very next day. I was diagnosed with severe endometriosis with adhesions spiderwebbing throughout my pelvic area. The after effects of the operation were traumatic. I was sent on my way with a Panadol. I was given no forewarning about the post-operative sharp stabbing pains in my shoulder. Each time I breathed trapped gas would be released like hot knives and catapult towards their target. It was as if I was being crucified.

Six months later, I landed in Australia. At my first checkup with a new specialist, I was told I had endometriosis—again. I was horrified and devastated. This progressive and debilitating disease was overgrowing like ivy around my organs. The female reproductive system and chronic pain doth not make dinner table conversations. Thoughts of infertility began to fester. It took another six months before I could face another operation. I only agreed after assurance that I would be admitted overnight, with pain relief on tap. From that point onwards, I would try and seek alternative methods of pain management, anything to prevent me from returning to the operating table.

No Full Stops

All things considered; our son was a little miracle.

His father and I moved in together and began nesting for his arrival. Two years later, we were blessed a second time, with a daughter and life just got busier. Cracks in our relationship appeared early, but I put our struggles down to juggling two young children. I revelled in the joy of motherhood and work. My multitasking skills were at least on point.

From the outside, we were a picture-perfect family. Over time though, the gap in our interests began to widen like the Grand Canyon. I felt his passion for triathlons and iron man competitions had taken precedence over our family. I would watch his races from the sidelines whilst wrangling a baby in a pram and a toddler who was forever running off. Training schedules began to take over his weekends, while I was left with the children for longer and longer stretches. I felt like I was already solo parenting. I used to joke that I would have to leave him because he looked better in Lycra than I did. He probably still does.

Our relationship slowly crumbled in increments invisible to the naked eye. I felt I was walking on eggshells. I needed to work through whether I was feeling signs of postnatal depression or something more profound. I originally stated that I didn't want him to propose just because I was pregnant. After two children and five years together and still no proposal, the writing was on the wall. My mother would always say, 'You have to be able to look at yourself in the mirror and know you have done your best'. I felt I was running out of steam with my efforts to get us back on track.

On our last family holiday abroad my sister aptly remarked, 'he just doesn't get you'. It was time. I could pretend no longer. I didn't want Mr Mac to model this behaviour or Miss Lipstick to mistake complacency for love. After living through the long and contentious divorce of my own parents and seeing them unhappy for so long, I didn't want that for our children. It would be years before I realised I also deserved better. It was a slow and painful process. I was supported by my family and started to make plans.

A stand-off ensued regarding who would leave the family home. I rented a small, two-bedroom apartment from a friend. It was 10 minutes away and near Bondi Beach. The law at the time did not recognise a de facto relationship equal to marriage, so we agreed on a nominal amount to cover the moving costs and rental bond. The moving day was long and fraught. I was so grateful to have some girlfriends help make the transition as smooth as it could be. The following week I collapsed with pneumonia. My body was grieving for me.

We settled into our new family dynamic. Yet it became apparent we were still not on the same parenting page. The search for our son's diagnosis of Asperger's syndrome was the source of dissension. I would send medical reports and letters from support teams and therapists, in a futile attempt to align our views. I hoped we could be worthy advocates. Instead, we became adversaries. This not only protracted the diagnostic process, but it also made co-parenting challenging. Detailed record keeping and intense conflict resulted. I fiercely protected the children, and in the process, became a spiralling vortex of emotions. I did not know how to establish boundaries and lacked any good self-care practices to keep me grounded. My energy was scattered. I was persistently in a 'fight, flight or defend' mode. This is without taking into account all the other crazy day-to-day logistics that come with single parenthood.

In 2012, a year after Mr Mac was diagnosed, I sought ways to provide some stability. The option to move to the countryside provided a solution but also proved antagonistic. I waved letters from specialists like white flags. Objections rained down like arrows from the opposition. The situation escalated and two days before our move, I was required to attend mediation. My nerves were shot. I was urged to negotiate complicated court orders, logistics, access arrangements and high school selections, all in the one sitting. There still was no agreement on our son's diagnosis or medications. It was a minefield of fine detail to comb through. The expectation was these revised agreements were to be delivered on the Friday—the same day that the removal trucks were pulling up. I felt cornered.

I don't know how I would have managed our relocation, both physically and emotionally, if it wasn't for the rallying of the mums from Bondi. They helped pack boxes in the weeks leading up to our move and coordinated removalists at both ends. This allowed me to rush around signing rental contracts, collecting keys, school uniforms and other sundries. I even missed my own leaving party as I was so tied up in legal paperwork and packing boxes. The children were taken out for dinner and cared for in my absence. I stayed put, glued to my computer and reeling from all the pages. Despite the endless nights of worry and checklists, I kept the reason for the move clear in my sight—the children. I had unwavering faith this move would benefit the whole family. From living in a constant state of destructive doubt and fear, this was the first proactive step I took to change that. I was determined to turn this ship around.

After two moving trucks and a full weekend of unpacking, I was ready to welcome the children to our new family home. They started their new school the following day. I was delighted to see how easily they settled in. It wasn't long before our family started to find its new rhythm and become part of the local school and community.

In 2014, my pelvic pain returned after enjoying some respite during those early child-rearing years. I feared that my endometriosis was back with a vengeance. I decided I had been in survival mode too long and now had more headspace to finally invest in my wellbeing. I was a woman on a mission and wanted to research a multitude of options to improve my health. My stomach was bloated. I had a niggling feeling that something ominous was afoot. Ever since I had become a single parent, the daily mixture of overwhelm and exhaustion had taken a toll. I interpreted this as penance for leaving their father. I told myself simply 'suck it up, princess'. I was prescribed antidepressants which kept me upright and functioning. I didn't want anyone to know though, fearing it would look like I was failing motherhood, or that it would be used against me. My 'happy pills' helped keep my anxiety at arm's length. They also prevented me from processing my turbulent emotions or feeling the inevitable breakdown of my body.

I approached my doctor with my concerns. Thankfully, she too was keen to get to the root cause. She had been our family doctor for a while. Over time, her role as my doctor had begun to shift. I began to see her more as Dr Familiar and a sounding board. A plethora of medical tests occurred as we began to unravel the tangled thread of symptoms. I initially thought my swollen stomach was an indicator of cervical cancer. We ruled that out. I was now eligible for free breast screening, so we tagged that on. The results were negative.

The pursuit of further tests for additional bone aches and pains were at this time temporarily halted. My father had been diagnosed with terminal lung cancer. I had not seen him for about five years. My elder sister gifted me some 'Airmiles' (frequent flying points) so that I could return to England in April 2014. I was due to go back for a quick holiday later that September, but we were unsure how long he would be with us. The trip allowed me to spend precious time with him, and a chance to get closure on some painful issues that lay between us.

When I returned home, the tests resumed. Coincidently, the bone scan detailed a type of osteoarthritis with secondary associations for lung cancer. I was fortunate that those results also came back negative. The gamut of tests had been extensive and woven in between the quest to find a new job and care for our new puppy, a black Labrador called Daisy. When life gives you lemons … get a puppy. At least that's our family motto.

My organisational skills honed over the years with legal papers, child support and school applications, meant I applied the same methodology to my medical history. I collated all past operations, scans, ultrasounds, and X-ray reports and neatly filed them in an A4 lever arch file with coloured tabs. I approached my health like a firefighter. Allocating resources only at times of emergency. Once each health crisis was averted rather than pause amongst the debris, I would simply move on—no time to look back. I was as detached from the findings as I was to the event. I had no mental capacity to connect the dots yet. I left the thinking to the experts. I never considered that I was the expert of my own body.

As a single parent, time vs. resources is a constant battle. I would look for ways to streamline efforts whilst simultaneously juggling multiple projects. I was busy at all times, just surviving and ensuring life's full plates continued spinning. My most noteworthy achievement during this time was keeping the children alive—literally. My son, undiagnosed at that time, would run off down the street and towards cars at any given moment. There were two children, so I always felt outnumbered. I would rely on taking only short trips out or organising meetups with friends in secure playgrounds and parks.

With my family living abroad and in different time zones, I was grateful to be able to create a support network on the ground. This included a tribe of mothers, friends and community to bolster us. However, even with this in place, I was still emotionally and physically depleted. There was never enough time or headspace for constructive thoughts or a chance to fully recalibrate. I was hypervigilant and my nervous system took a pounding. The only time there was any reprieve was, if and when, the children would visit their father. I would either spend my free time completing housework, sleeping, clutching a glass of wine or having a sporadic reflexology session. I just needed to remain upright and get through the day. Our bedtime ritual would stretch out for hours and by the time everyone kept in their beds for more than ten minutes, I would dive gratefully into mine. We'd made it through another day.

Of course, I forever hoped that projects would magically disappear. In reality, I would either be overloaded, overwhelmed, or just plain over it. I learned how to keep the children engaged or motivated by telling them stories. It could get them to eat, sit at the table, stay in a queue, or simply keep their seatbelt on. I adopted an English aristocrats 'spare and heir' approach to meal preparation: doubling the recipes to ensure one meal for now and a spare to freeze. I always needed a few aces up my sleeve; I couldn't rely on just going with the flow. Those youthful days of abandon were long gone. Now, structure was my saviour and my overlord. Funny to think that it was also my comfort.

I would prepare packed lunch ingredients ahead of time (carrots and cucumbers cut and stored in water in the fridge). This was before meal prep was a thing, although I doubt mine would ever be Instagram worthy. I'd learnt to adapt and drop myself from the equation. I had a few other timesaving hacks such as my fondly named 'car wash' shower. I would aim to get my hair and body wet, soaped, and rinsed as if I had five people simultaneously working on me. This may have inadvertently contributed to water-saving. More importantly, it ensured I'd be finished before needing to prise the children from each other, as they argued over toys, drinks, attention, or space. Thank God they weren't both girls as they might have fought over clothes too.

In late 2014, after returning from England the second time, we revisited my discomfort and painful endometriosis-type symptoms again. I was booked to have some exploratory surgery the following April with Dr Practical. Finally, a female surgeon. She took a no-nonsense approach. I had conceded it was unlikely I would have any more children and gave consent for her to do 'whatever was necessary'. The last thing I wanted was to be woken up just to provide consent to having further surgery. At this stage, a partial hysterectomy would be required to ease symptoms.

I decided to multitask my surgeries like my other chores. If I had to take time out for one operation, why not make it two? I booked a second surgeon to come and repair an umbilical hernia at the same time. He was Dr Thorough. Measured and calm in his approach. Serious, but warm. Organising two surgeons to be available for the same operating date and time was an achievement on its own. Getting the green light to have parenting duties covered was nothing short of miraculous.

One thing was for sure, I was going to be match fit, and this was the reason I had attended CrossFit in the first place. I was aiming to have the shortest post-op recovery on record. I was thorough in my approach and booked an appointment with a local naturopath. I relayed my sorry health history and was given a bountiful collection of supplements and nutritional advice, which I followed diligently. I was still fatigued, though. I put that down to my ongoing concerns about how I would manage during the post-op recovery period—no driving for six weeks or heavy lifting. I had never been so physically hampered before and knew it would majorly impact my ability to do things with and for the children. On the upside, it would mean I would literally be the 'stay at home' mum which I had always aspired to be.

In the first few weeks of the year, we had completed the usual 'back to school' preparations for the first term. Shoes, bags, books and stationery had all been bought. Now, I needed to bring forward and complete all possible appointments required during the post-op period—swimming club, school support team meetings, children's dental appointments, applications for high school choices and arranging interviews. It was a military-style operation. The logistics were meticulously planned with no room for error. Being a family of Pisces, back-to-back children's birthday parties also needed to be arranged. One, a home-based crafting party at the end of February, tick. The other, an outdoor insect party in early March, tick. Miss Lipstick was turning nine and Mr Mac was turning eleven. I even managed to squeeze a Saturday night out celebration for reaching my 44th year, tick. Quite exhausting, but somehow it all got done. 12 days of Christmas was child's play compared to 12 weeks of this kind of event planning.

I moved through my to-do list reasonably smoothly during those months, all while continuing my new active regime and additional health supplements. However, I couldn't shake feeling extremely tired or get through one day without a nana nap.

The Sunday following my birthday celebrations, I woke with a throbbing ear infection in my right ear. I attributed it to being rundown and assumed I would probably just need some trusty antibiotics, to knock it on the head. It seemed a small price to pay for having some fun. The first available appointment I could find online was the following day. I planned to be in and out to collect the script. Perhaps I should have paid more attention to the date—it was Sunday, 'The Ides of March'.

If God made the world in seven days, mine was about to collapse in just five.

2

Cup of Tea?

Monday 16th March 2015

I'd never met this particular doctor before. He was warm, friendly and considerate—Dr Compassionate, if you will. After a few minutes of the usual back-and-forth questions, I had a script in hand. I had barely risen from my chair to leave when I felt an overwhelming urge to scratch my right breast. I continued to make my way to the door when something stopped me in my tracks. As I reached for the door handle, I paused and turned around to face Dr Compassionate once more.

'Oh, just before I go, I meant to ask, but I keep forgetting … Please, can you take a quick look at my right breast? It's been a bit itchy.'

He motioned me back into the room and ushered me to take my top off.

'Well, it doesn't *look* like breast cancer, but maybe your hormones are starting to drop,' he said matter-of-factly. 'I'll give you another script for some cream.'

It jarred that he'd even mentioned breast cancer. I remember smirking to myself and thinking, 'I doubt he could have X-ray eyes to make that prediction.' It felt odd that he even considered it an option. Just a couple of months before I had a breast check done by the nurse at my pap smear and nothing was mentioned. If he'd looked at my notes, he would also have seen that I'd had a mammogram this time last year. The mammogram report had clearly stated in bold **'there was no evidence of breast cancer.'** I knew the exact words as I had just filed it in my new health folder. Besides, I'd always had sensitive skin, so I thought no more about it. I duly took this second script and left for the pharmacy next door.

'It appears I'm dropping hormones left, right and centre,' I joked with the pharmacist as I passed over my scripts.

I returned straight home to catch up on my consulting project. It needed to be completed by the end of the following day. My mobile was on silent so that I could be fully focused on the task at hand. It wasn't until later that afternoon that I picked up his message, left at 2.15 pm.

'Ah hello, it's Dr Compassionate from earlier. I was just thinking about the itching that you are having and probably should do an ultrasound and a mammogram just to be sure that it's not something serious … I've left a form for you at the front desk if that's okay? And if you get that done … if there's any abnormality, I will give you a call and let you know. If it's normal, I won't call you.'

My first reaction was of slight annoyance. First, the ear infection now this. It felt like I was playing 'Whac-A-Mole' except I was the mole. Now I would have yet *another* thing to do. Why did he suddenly think of this *after* I left? Maybe he wasn't convinced that he had X-ray eyes after all. But, whatever the reason, and I never found out exactly what prompted him to call, I will be forever grateful that he did.

There was a free appointment the very next morning at the local X-ray place in town. Not only that, but I was able to have back-to-back appointments starting first thing in the morning. I'd be done and dusted by lunchtime and ready to meet my deadline. #Winning. That's the beauty of living in a country town, you don't have to wait for weeks to get appointments. I didn't have time to think anything more about it, as I could hear the noisy chatter outside of the children getting off the bus. Another reason to be grateful for small towns, a door-to-door school bus service. I just didn't know how much of a lifesaver that would be.

Tuesday 17th March 2015

The next day began with the usual pre-school chaos.

'Come on. Get up now … Hurry up … It shouldn't take that long to put your socks on … Put your iPad down and come and eat your breakfast … *Yes*, you can have four pieces of toast.' (*You can have a chocolate bar as long as you eat something*, I muttered under my breath.)

Hurried mothers up and down the land relay the same endless stream of commands and demands before school starts. Day in and day out, our children look at us as if it's the first time they've ever heard they must wear shoes—a perpetual Groundhog Day. I've often wanted to record my words and play them on a loop.

'Quickly, grab your bags. Come on and hurry up, the bus will be here soon!' I pleaded.

They ran out the door, schoolbag straps falling off their shoulders and large school hats precariously perched on their heads.

'Zip your bag up, your water bottle is about to fall out!' I shouted exasperated.

Then, just as the doors of the bus opened, inviting them to board, I shouted out, 'Bye! Have a lovely day,' and waved them off. I desperately hoped that my last cheery sentence would erase all prior screeching from their minds. I would not yet realise how much I'd cling to the monotony of this morning routine. I glanced at the clock and haphazardly threw breakfast plates and bowls into the dishwasher. The sooner I got there, the sooner I got back, I reminded myself.

First up was the mammogram at 9.30 am.

I knew the drill. It's always such an intimate appointment. The mammographer needs to get up close and personal. She wrestled my boobs to get them placed delicately between two heavy slabs, approximately the weight of a couple of bricks.

'Right, just hold your breath now please, and keep very still.'

In between repositioning, I tried to find some common ground between us.

'Oh … are you a single mum also?'

'Now, hold your breath please and keep very still,' she continued.

I wondered if I was holding my breath sufficiently. It's a complex manoeuvre to clutch the machinery and remain motionless. I tried to find ways to distract myself from the discomfort of having my boobs squished. So much to think about. Thank God I was not born in an era where portraits were painted, I would never have been able to stand still that long.

I continued to chatter as if matching the invasion of my personal space with deeply prying questions put us on an even playing field. This lighthearted banter certainly made the examination time go by quickly. Or maybe she thought it slowed it down?

She wandered off to check the films and returned moments later.

'You can just get dressed now and return to the waiting room. Someone will call you for your next appointment.'

Hallelujah, we had some passable images.

The waiting room was filling up. I reflected on how I had been through a breast lump scare before. I'd found a lump in my right breast just after my daughter was born. It turned out to be nothing, literally. No lump was found by the time I had the appointment. They did, however, discover that I had cysts in my left breast. I'd already been told I had cysts in my uterus and around my ovaries. It seemed it was to be part of my body make-up. Better to have cysts than be a cissy, I thought. By my logic, if lightning doesn't strike twice, neither could a lump in my breasts.

'Alexandra James ... Alexandra James ... Alexandra James?'

'Oh, yes, sorry, that's me!' I shrilly replied.

I followed the sonographer down the corridor.

'Well, my first name is legally Alexandra, and my middle name is Louise, but I've always been called Louise. In fact, when I was born, I was going to be called Louise Mary … but then my father didn't want me to be called that, so I was christened Alexandra Louise, but I was always called Lulu growing up. Here in Australia, everything has to match your birth certificate and passport, so everything is listed that way, but I'm called Louise, so I'm afraid I'm not used to being called Alexandra. I even have to tell them at the hospital to call me Louise in the recovery room, or I might not respond!' I breathlessly tried to explain. Too much information Louise, too much information.

She nodded politely and lead me into the ultrasound room.

Stop chatting too much, I berated myself. Even I was surprised at this relentless stream of words. My inner pep talk didn't last too long. I now had turned my attention to the ultrasound monitor. It took me back to the first time I tried to spot a baby amongst the murky black and white imagery on screen. My curiosity is hard to quench.

'Sorry if it's cold,' she said, squeezing the bottle from a great height above. A blob of clear, cold gel fell onto my right breast, causing me to flinch. She grabbed the handheld paddle and started to move it around my breast in clockwise movements. Before I felt substantial pressure on any one area, she would move the paddle to the next. This procedure did not hold the same level of discomfort as the mammogram, and it didn't require me to hold my breath. Her face moved between the screen and the paddle. My eyes darted between her face, the screen, and my body. There appeared to be no furrows on her forehead that I could detect. I took this as a good sign. She turned her attention to my left breast.

As I repositioned, I realised I would now enjoy an unobstructed view of the screen. I felt my body ease. It was just a matter of completing this final examination and ticking it off today's checklist. Now that I was more relaxed, so too was my need to fill the silence.

'You know, they've found cysts before in my left breast, at 10 o'clock and 12 o'clock,' I added jovially, trying to catch her eyes. 'I wonder what time it will be this time?' I said with a smirk. She continued, unaffected by my sorry attempts at humour. My mind began to drift as I started thinking about how similar this was to the school playground game of 'What's the Time Mr Wolf?' I stifled a laugh. She put down her tools. But, as I waited for the ceremonial wipe down and my marching orders, the atmosphere in the room shifted.

'I'm just going to get the doctor, please wait here,' she uttered gently.

I've watched too many daytime movies to know no good can come from those words. I sat up on the bed, waiting for her to return. I had the temporary gown still on just in case they needed to do another ultrasound—at least the gel had warmed up now. I'd been texting and joking back and forth with a friend between appointments to pass the time. I didn't feel like being funny anymore.

The sonographer reappeared at the door. She was alone.

'We'd like to get another mammogram image, just so that we can have all the information together,' she proffered without explaining the doctor's absence. 'Would you like a cup of tea?' she added.

It was with those three words—**Cup of tea?**—my eyes pricked with tears. Any English person will tell you that being offered a cup of tea usually means you were about to be delivered some excruciating and unbearable news. I sat back in the waiting room and surveyed the room. I was the only one with a cup of tea in hand.

'Alexandra James?'

'Yes.' This time, I was ready. A different mammographer led me back into the mammography room. I went back through the motions—arms up, squeeze and hold your breath. Change position. Repeat.

I returned to the waiting room and wondered if this would be the last time that I would have to take my clothes off today. I had been here for nearly five hours. All plans for the day were wiped from my mind as I sat silently, avoiding all eye contact. I couldn't even muster up enough energy to get up and chase the ultrasound and mammogram films.

The first mammographer noticed me still sitting in the waiting room. Thank God she did, or I may have just stayed there till closing time.

'Are you still waiting?' she gently asked.

'Yes, I am,' I said quietly and looked down again.

I watched as she walked to reception and searched for my results. She returned to hand them over to me. She held on to my elbow for just a little longer than felt normal.

Cup of Tea?

'Take care of yourself,' she quietly added.

I slunk off home. I was barely through the door before I ripped open the large, sealed envelope. It contained just the films. The reports would be sent directly to the doctor. It was as if they knew what I would do. I held the films up against the window, towards the light. It was my cheap alternative to those viewing lightboxes doctors used in TV shows. I looked at them with novice eyes, eagerly looking for any notable signs or clues. I even googled 'cups of tea and mammogram' desperately looking for answers. Would you believe that 'crescent-shaped teacups' is such a thing in a mammogram?

That night, I wrote an email to my family about being given a cup of tea. I was afraid my family would think I was overreacting as I hadn't got all the facts yet. I tried to sound positive.

'I'm hoping this was just good country hospitality, but I haven't had that treatment at previous scans,' I wrote.

Somehow, even then, I knew.

3

Needlepoint

Wednesday 18th March 2015

It took just one day for the written reports to be sent back. The receptionist at the doctor's surgery called.

'Hello Louise, we have your results. There will also be an additional form to pick up as you'll need to book in for a fine needle biopsy. All the details are on the back of the form,' she added, making it all seem quite straightforward.

I put the phone down. The word **biopsy** rang through my ears. I tried to focus on the words 'fine needle' to make it seem less daunting. I conjured up images of Victorian ladies by the fireplace, doing cross-stitch.

I decided, rather than let the children catch the bus back from school that day, I would collect them. I'd get the paperwork on the way home. Looking back now, I'm not sure if it was either for distraction or to prevent me from falling apart. By the time I'd reached the school, I'd convinced myself that this was not an uncommon procedure and probably precautionary. I've had to deal with worse—just another bump in the road.

The children remained in the car whilst I popped into the reception. I would usually chat and joke around with the staff, but this time, I just wanted to be as quick as I could. Back in the car, I hesitated before ripping open yet another sealed envelope. The children were happily chatting between themselves in the back of the car. I quickly scanned the paperwork. It was full of jargon words, numbers, and figures that I couldn't decipher, until the final paragraph. The words jumped off the page.

'Mass, 1 o'clock … **highly worrisome for malignancy.**'

I was transfixed by the words. This wasn't a fun game of Mr Wolf any longer. Perhaps I thought that by staring at the page long enough, the words would magically change. I was glad that I was in the front seat so the children couldn't see my face.

The letters started to lift off the page and move in and out of focus. Had I read them correctly? The context was key. If the word 'worrisome' had been found in a Jane Eyre novel, it would sound rather genteel. It's close proximity to the word 'malignancy' here, made it more dastardly than dainty. I would have to wait until later to google those terms and find their true significance. There would be no sugar coating it this time.

'Is it hot in here?' I opened the window. My heart started beating out of my chest like a cartoon. Could this *really* be life-threatening? What will happen to the children? Oh my god, the children …

Before my thoughts started to spiral further, I was interrupted by an increase in noise and restlessness from the back seat.

'Why are we *still* here … Why aren't we going home?'

'Just be quiet!' I snapped … I needed time to think.

What should I be doing? What do I do now? I was in a circle of confusion. All my problem-solving skills left through the open car window. I searched for the other form. Just book the appointment. Get an appointment. It was the only thing I could think to do.

'Where's my mobile?' It could have been in my hand for all the focus I could rally at the time. A sense of urgency was increasing as I searched the front seats. It was as if we would never be able to leave that car park until I had made that call.

When I finally spoke to the receptionist, I stumbled over my words and was put on hold. She must have sensed my distress, as she managed to squeeze me in for a fine needle biopsy the very next day.

After the appointment had been made, there was nothing more to do except drive us home. For me the unknown was paralysing. Everything else faded into the background. Thankfully the children were blissfully unaware of what was going on. I cleared all my planned appointments for the next day, including my son's high school interview. I don't remember what reason I gave him for the change, but he didn't ask any further questions. For the children, tomorrow would be just another school day and another wave goodbye.

I'd get good at this pretence.

Thursday 19th March 2015

I had asked my friend Audrey to come with me to the appointment. I didn't know her really well at the time, but I knew that she would be calm and not curl into a foetal position at the first hurdle. It was the first time I had reached out for support. I'd realised I would need some help with the logistics of getting back and forth to appointments. More importantly I would need the emotional support. I just couldn't do this on my own and then present a together version of myself for the children. I was a house of cards.

'If they start telling you *anything*, just ask for me to come in so that I can hear it too,' Audrey suggested as we waited for the biopsy. It was the best advice I'd been given. I couldn't trust my ability to process information anymore. I feared I had already reached capacity. Like a character from a Charlie Brown cartoon, I only heard 'Blah Blah Blah'.

My name was called. I immediately got up. I was on autopilot when I changed into the dark blue throwaway gown. I sat in the side cubicle, wringing my hands until I was finally called into the ultrasound room. I was greeted by a familiar face, the sonographer from a few days prior. The last time I had been here, there was a carousel of operators. Just to have the same one twice put me at ease.

'I'll be assisting the doctor today,' she said. I'm unsure if it was her ultrasounds that prompted the second mammogram or in combination with the first mammogram. Either way, she had been part of the diagnostic team. I was dying to ask her if she already knew I might have cancer when she had offered me that cup of tea. This really wasn't the time for my curiosity.

The doctor performing the fine needle biopsy entered the room. She was very efficient and focused on the task at hand. There would be no joking around today. The doctor had a thick Eastern European accent. I could barely understand what she was saying about the procedure, which in hindsight, was probably best.

The thin needle she was going to use didn't look quite as small and dainty as my imagined Victorian ladies would use. I watched the screen as the needle was carefully eased into my skin and entered the lump. I would like to say it was an inner strength that prevented me from flinching or moving, but looking back, it was because I was so disconnected from my own body and emotions. It was as if I was watching someone else on the screen. An experience I now know is often triggered by severe stress and trauma. At the time a blessing in disguise, but something I would need to address later on.

At the end of the procedure, I began asking questions. As the doctor started to answer, I remembered Audrey's parting words. I was already straining to understand and didn't want to miss anything vital, so I asked if Audrey could come in. We waited for her to join us. The doctor then resumed.

'Preeparrrrree for cancer,' she almost purred the words.

It was the first time the C-word was uttered. Up until then, I'd felt like everyone else knew more. Hushed tones, averted eyes, and closed-door conversations had led me to this point. I now wanted some clarity and to be in the driver's seat—even if it was in a rusty secondhand car with no steering wheel.

'Could it be fibroids?' asked Audrey, trying to offer up alternative options. I admired her for not allowing the doctor off the hook so quickly. I sat disturbingly still as the information poured slowly over me like hot wax. The doctor offered to rush through the report so we would have our answers.

We left without any sealed envelopes. All we could do was reconvene at the nearest coffee shop to compare notes and try and make sense of what we had just heard. That's the thing about a cancer diagnosis, it comes at you one fragment of information at a time. When you don't know the type, stage, or extent of what you might have, everyone is in the same boat—the sinking boat of terror, confusion, and fear. The fragility of not knowing is juxtaposed with the comfort of not knowing. There is something blissful and peaceful in ignorance. I should have appreciated that more.

They say if it looks like a duck and quacks like a duck, then it's … cancer. What type of cancer and if it's just been living in one pond or has been swimming elsewhere was still unknown.

4

Facebook Official

Friday 20th March 2015

Ironic that it was Harmony Day at the children's school when my life felt anything but. I was grateful for the added distraction of getting everyone in the right attire for their chosen nation. My daughter was dressed in a beret, plaits, and a French T-shirt, representing my mother's ancestors—France. Mr Mac was wearing a red Fred Perry shirt and shorts and represented the lesser-known Dinosaur Country.

The phone rang. It was the receptionist from the doctor's surgery. 'Hi Louise, just confirming that you have an appointment booked this afternoon to review your biopsy results. We wondered if you would prefer to have a female doctor instead?'

'Oh, okay, thanks,' I replied. There wasn't any particular reason why I agreed, but it seemed that if I was going to cry, best do it in female company. It was also my first clue to anticipate the worst.

In the absence of any family living in Australia, I had asked Hope, another English friend, to come with me. I needed some familiarity from the past. We had been housemates in London in our 20s. As fate would have it, we had bumped into each other at the dog park in Bowral, Australia more than twenty years later. It amazes me how the universe reunited us just at the right time. I needed this hopeful sign.

In the waiting room, I kept getting distracted with my new game 'Reading Faces'. I would try to make eye contact with the reception staff each time they looked up to catch hints that they had seen my results. I couldn't sit still. Dr Compassionate glanced over at me as he called in another patient then darted back into his office. I wanted to get up and tell him it wasn't anything personal that I'd agreed to a female doctor this time, but I remained seated. If I had no control of my jittery legs sitting, I didn't want to test them out by standing.

A female doctor, new to the practice, warmly greeted us and ushered us into her room. I duly sat in the seat next to her table with Hope on the other side of me. I clenched my hands, awaiting the verdict. It felt a bit anticlimactic as the written histology report had not yet been received. Disappointment swept over me. This was being strung out like an episode of *The Bold and the Beautiful*. A knock on the door and Dr Compassionate popped his head in.

'Hi, I saw you come into the waiting room. I've been watching all day to see if the results had come in,' he added.

'I bet that's the medical equivalent of watching bids on eBay,' I joked in an attempt to lighten the mood.

There was a slight pause.

'I'm afraid it is **cancer**,' he said.

I floated out of my body and hovered above. Hope took the details in and started to ask questions. I watched from afar. I heard the exchange of voices, but they seemed distant. I wanted to take charge and dispute the news.

'I'm sorry cancer? I think you've made a mistake. I'm booked to deal with other medical issues. May I suggest you have the wrong address? My new health folder with the coloured tabs—it doesn't have room for this extra information.' But I sat in silence.

Dr Compassionate said his goodbyes and left the room. The conversation turned to the next steps.

'Do you have a breast surgeon?' the doctor gently enquired.

'No,' I said bewildered. 'Ummm well … the surgeon who I am booked to have an umbilical hernia with, Dr Thorough, I think he does breast surgery?' I added coyly.

I remembered he had the words 'General Surgeon' and 'Breast Surgeon' listed underneath his name on the shiny brass plaque outside his office. Perhaps not quite the best referral I'd ever used, but I was desperate to leave the room and catch my breath. I probably would have agreed to anyone or anything at that moment.

'Well, let's call him to get an appointment for early next week,' she replied and made the call. Practical and logical action. This was exactly what I needed.

An appointment was made with Dr Thorough for the following Monday. It was not the best news to start the weekend, but at least I had a couple of days to get used to the information. I was not sure *how* or *if* I should tell the children.

Hope guided me back to her car. Thankfully, I hadn't driven myself as I was still in shock. I had wished that we might have avoided this fuss and would be given a last-minute reprieve.

'No cup of tea this time … let's get some wine,' offered Hope. 'Do you want anything else?' she added, taking charge.

'Crisps please,' I replied feebly. They were always my comfort food of choice. I wasn't sure how much they would help this time.

'You shouldn't be alone tonight,' Hope added. 'Is there anyone who can come over after I have to leave?'

'I'm not sure,' I hesitantly replied. My mind appeared to be on a processing time delay. I knew that I wouldn't be alone that night as the children would be returning on the school bus shortly. But I needed to be surrounded by an adult circle of support as the aftershock wore off. I needed to buffer my thoughts from deteriorating. So, I sent a text to a couple of friends to come over while Hope went to buy supplies. I couldn't face bumping into people, so I stayed in the car. I was grateful she had parked in the underground car park.

I suddenly recognised one of the mums from school walk past the car. Before I knew why, I had leapt out of the car. I had this sudden urge to tell someone. Anyone. I didn't know her very well, but it seemed that I needed a practice conversation before I could tell anyone else or my family.

I stopped her in her tracks. We exchanged the usual pleasantries and surface-level conversations. Then I awkwardly blurted out, 'I just found out I've got cancer'.

I remember my father doing something similar the year before. I was dealing with the after-effects of Mr Mac's emergency appendectomy and readmittance to the hospital. And while I was gathering things to return to the hospital, my father called on Skype. He asked how Mr Mac was feeling. As I was answering, he suddenly interrupted and announced he had lung cancer. His news was totally out of the blue. It was the first time he had volunteered any information. It was as if he had no control over when, how, or what he said.

Now here I was, all my best intentions to avoid the same scenario, had abandoned me. At the very first glimpse of a human walking past, I was ready to bare my soul.

After I blurted out my own diagnosis, there was a moment of discomfort as nothing else was said. I'm not sure what reaction I expected, but I was relieved when finally, the school mum responded, 'Oh, I must dash … I'm already late for school pick up,' and off she went.

Had she heard me properly? Was the enormity of the situation somehow lost in translation? Or did she really not know what to say?

Feeling slightly rejected, I retreated back into the car to wait for Hope. This prepared me for the many unusual responses people provide when they are confronted with bad news. The first response is usually shock and overwhelm as they grapple with the information and shortly followed by fear at what it might mean to their lives. It was hard not to take it personally at the time. On reflection, there is no one right way to respond to the news, especially when you are accosted with it.

That night, I drank wine with my friends, and later, on my own. I sent an email to my family with an update. I couldn't face calls as speaking those words might make it more real. I was worried the children would hear my conversations and that I might wobble. Best keep the lid on my emotions secured. I needed time to process before I could let the children know.

It was far easier to put things in writing. Better to relay information as a transaction of words than to connect inwards and feel. I just didn't have the capacity for that yet ... I became a master of contradiction. I decided I would just take the bull by the horns and release the information into the world in one fell swoop. I made it 'Facebook official'.

I could only muster five words. I posted, 'Let the cancer journey begin'.

Somehow, I needed to feel a connection at a time when I felt most alone. Or maybe, I needed others to feel for me when I could not. I poured another glass of wine. I wanted to numb my emotions.

Don't poke the bear.

5

To Be or Not to Be Cancer?

There wasn't much time to dwell on the news as the children were with me that weekend. They were too young to have access to Facebook to see my big announcement. The responses from people to my post were warm and supportive. It was as if I needed an outside perspective to the news to help me digest or garner my own view. I had the emotional range of a child—looking to others for permission to feel. There was no time now for a pity party. There were children's parties to attend, housework to be conquered, and washing stops for no-one. The normality of the weekend was in stark contrast to the gravity of my impending situation. I snatched moments alone when I could. I was a pressure cooker releasing traces of steam behind my closed bedroom door. I didn't know how to explain to the children what was happening. I didn't want them to feel my confusion and anxiety, so I packed my emotions back up into a box and buried it deep. It became my very own perverse hidden treasure.

My elder sister had advised me not to tell the children anything. I assume she felt this would shield them. I had always been open and honest with them, perhaps some might say too honest. Maybe I was overcompensating for my own feelings of not always being seen or heard growing up. I always strived for my children to feel that they could trust me to hold their secrets, be non-judgemental and to love them unconditionally. Not always easy to do in practice when you are tired or not feeling present. People were also coming in and out of the house so it would be impossible to hide the news for long. I felt it was better that they heard something directly from me. I was worried if they worked it out for themselves, our trust might be broken, and they'd become wary that I was keeping other things hidden. By now, they would have heard bits and bobs of conversations from the stream of visitors in and out. I would need to choose my time wisely. It would need to be soon.

Monday 23rd March 2015

I was relieved it was finally Monday and time to touch base with Dr Thorough. He would now be responsible for removing the cancer. I always called it 'The' cancer as if it had a formal and distant relationship from myself. I could only think of it as singular and separate to my body—an accidental tourist visiting one site only and not a global traveller.

Dr Thorough's office was masculine with dark wood and black leather furnishings and a large desk taking up the majority of the room. There was a bed for examinations set up against the wall on the other side, and seating for two carefully placed in front of the desk. Dr Thorough sat in a large, high-backed, black leather, padded office chair. It reminded me of the one used in the English quiz show *Mastermind*. Behind him were impressive bookshelves filled with some books interspersed with frames of his wife and children.

It was strange to be switching gears from discussions of a simple umbilical hernia repair to the removal of 'a' or 'potentially spreading' cancer. At least I had already met with him once before, so that was one less unknown to deal with.

Audrey also came to this appointment for moral support. It was reassuring to have someone by my side to simultaneously hear the news and discuss and compare our different perspectives afterwards. The written biopsy report lay on the desk in front of him. We weren't privy to what it said, but he seemed dismissive of its contents.

'I think we should get another biopsy done,' he announced.

'*What?*' I asked in horror and perhaps a few octaves higher than necessary. 'But I was told it was cancer on Friday … I've put it up on Facebook … Are you saying I might not have cancer?' My mind was racing—oh my God, oh my God. I don't have cancer? I could almost hear my family saying, 'We knew you were being overdramatic'. Oh my God, what is everyone else going to say? I'd had so many beautiful messages of support over the weekend. I could feel a flush of colour on my cheeks. I looked over at Audrey in horror. Yes, not in excitement or glee, but in horror!

'I'm not necessarily saying that you don't have cancer … but let's get another sample taken. A core biopsy, this time to get more information.' He was methodical in his response, neither wanting to get my hopes up nor concur with the cancer diagnosis.

He must have seen the tinge of embarrassment on my face as he told me he never used Facebook but ended with a warning. '*Do Not* put anything else up on Facebook until we know more.'

I felt chastised.

'No … umm, no I won't put anything more up, I promise,' I relented.

He handed over the referral form and told me to arrange an appointment for a new biopsy to be taken at the hospital this time. If I hadn't had Hope with me the previous Friday, I would have thought I'd dreamt it all up and was going a bit mad. As we reached the car park, the receptionist called and asked me to come back into his office.

'I know you would like to get this done as soon as possible, but I would like you to wait an extra day so you can see a particular doctor who works on Wednesday. I'd like him to take the next sample.' Dr Thorough instructed.

Wow, this sounded doubly cautious. The venue would now be different. The person taking the samples would be different—his preferred doctor. He must really not trust those initial results. My head was spinning, so we went straight back to my house to regroup. Another bottle of wine opened. Well, it was 5pm somewhere else in the world. It felt like deja vu, except this time, we were celebrating that I might not have cancer. Thank God I hadn't told the children yet.

I started to reel again that I might not have cancer after all. I sheepishly turned to Audrey …

'Oh God, what if people think I'm like the lady in the news who told everyone she had brain cancer and she didn't ... people are going to think I'm a fraud if I don't have cancer.'

'*No-one* is going to get annoyed and say that you are a terrible person for *not* having cancer,' she reassured me.

It was almost as though having cancer was more acceptable than admitting I might have jumped the gun and got it wrong. I poured another glass of wine. I didn't want to allow any further insights to formulate. I was not ready to be a hostage to my thoughts again. Too much thinking time makes Louise a very anxious girl.

Wednesday 25th March 2015

Fortunately, I had been given a last-minute consultancy project that required a collation of research. It was not too taxing and made the intervening day pass quicker.

I felt like the 70s Harmony Hairspray TV commercial '*is* she, or *isn't* she?' but with cancer. I didn't know the exact differences between the two biopsies. There had been a differing opinion on why I didn't just have a core biopsy in the first place. I was told this one would hurt more and sting like a bee. It would take two larger samples than the first.

Audrey came with me to this appointment too. We were taken into a room to wait for the doctor's arrival. I wanted to make sure Audrey was there from the start of the appointment to avoid anything being missed or misunderstood. I started making small talk as the sonographer set up.

'I'm getting a bit concerned that my friend here has seen more of my boobs than anyone else I know!' I joked. Inappropriate jokes again Louise.

The doctor came through the door. Before he'd even had time to introduce himself, I blurted out, 'We've been *waiting* for you!'

'Sorry If I'm late,' he responded with an apologetic look on his face.

Another failed attempt to lighten the room (or just my anxiety).

'Oh, no … umm … I mean we were asked by Dr Thorough to *wait* until you were available to perform the biopsy. Dr Thorough wanted to make sure this sample was only taken by you.' I feebly added this compliment at the end.

Audrey sat in the far corner of the room, watching the sonographer on the keyboard. I was lying on my side so that my 1 o'clock position could be easily reached. This required an arm stretched above my head. Of course, my lump placement would be in an awkward position. I kept myself distracted by watching the screen and analysing the different needle techniques. The sensation of a cold, steel, wide needle (or as I like to call it 'fat needle') being inserted, is not for the faint-hearted. My ability to disengage from my body and become pliable ragdoll at moments like these, was well-practised. My high pain threshold (together with a single dose of Panadol beforehand) would serve me well. However, it was my ability to simultaneously shut down my mind that got me over the line. It was as if my emotions were spelled with a silent 'e'. I could logically speculate the feeling of pain, but not fully feel it or be consumed by it. My mind and body were severed parts of me. Their disconnection kept me safe.

To Be or Not to Be Cancer?

Once it was clear I wouldn't need to be motionless anymore, I summoned up the courage to ask for some clarity from the doctor. 'Please, can I ask you something? I'm a bit confused!' He turned to look at me quizzically.

'Last Friday, I was told *I had cancer*,' (No Louise, please don't mention you put it up on Facebook) 'and when we saw Dr Thorough on Monday, he asked for a second biopsy to be done, as if maybe *I don't have cancer*? How can this be?'

The doctor looked at me sympathetically and explained.

'Louise, your first Mammogram/CT results were what we call 'Category **4**' while the histology report from your first biopsy was also 'Code **4**'.'

I slowly took in the information and then squealed in delight.

'Oh … 4 and 4??' I repeated, *'I'm 44!'* I declared proudly for making this correlation. I was desperately trying to make sense of it all. Clearly, I had no clue.

'No. What it means is that it is 95% *likely to be cancer*,' he added. 'The new results provide more of an idea about the type and stage of cancer; whether there are any cells from any other areas of the body present and how aggressive the cancer is.'

'Oh,' I replied.

'The results will take a couple of days,' he finished and left the room.

We retreated to yet another café, to exchange information. I updated Audrey on what the doctor had just said while she had been talking with the sonographer. It appeared as if I heard A, B, C. She heard X, Y, Z. We were either going to need reinforcements to get the full picture, record the conversation, or as we agreed, next time bring a notepad and pen.

The meeting with Dr Thorough for the results was booked for Friday, so we had a couple of days to prepare.

Thursday 26th March 2015

There's nothing like another dress-up day at school to keep your mind off of things. The 26th of March was a 'self-help' fundraising day at school. For the price of a gold coin, the children could wear non-school uniform clothes for the day and purchase homemade treats from their peers. Miss Lipstick chose to dress up like a spice girl with denim shorts and a sequined hat. Mr Mac had selected longer shorts and a top. He completed his look by wearing a horse head mask on his head. It was wonderful to see them both excited about something completely off-topic. I wished that I could dress up as someone else for the day and gorge on sweet treats.

Instead, I was back at the doctors. I had developed an itchy rash on my chest. My ear infection had now turned septic. I felt like the walking dead. I potentially was. My body breakdown was now externally visible. If it had felt unheard before, it appeared screaming now. Dr Familiar had returned from her holiday and was in disbelief at what had happened in just a week since I saw her. It was as if she had walked back into a warzone.

The second biopsy histology report was not yet with her. I asked her to print a copy of the first report and its **Code 4** status so that I could see it with my own eyes. There are many differences between codes, categories, stages, and types of cancers. It required speed learning to keep up with all these new terms. To this day, they still confuse me. It had been recommended that I have an MRI/CT to rule out other areas. I wondered if Dr Thorough would agree. I just wanted to skip ahead to the final diagnosis to have some certainty. I had been living in the unknown for less than two weeks and was already suffering a relentless thirst for assurance. I cannot imagine what other people must go through with longer timelines. I wanted to know *exactly* what I was dealing with. Safety in numbers was given a whole new meaning.

As I appeared to get tongue-tied around any surgeon, I took the opportunity to run over all the likely options, including the worst, with Dr Familiar. It was my practice run before meeting with Dr Thorough again, the next day. I would arrive fully prepared with my game face on. I knew I was capable of an ugly crying face; it just hadn't revealed itself yet. I didn't want him to be the first to see it. I wanted ours to be a professional relationship. My vulnerability was my jack-in-the-box. I feared not being able to close its lid again.

I was still on hold for the original partial hysterectomy and hernia repair operations due in a week. I had been avoiding the calls from hospital admissions to confirm the surgery details and surgeons attending. I was unsure of who would still attend, what they would be doing and was not ready to give up my allocated surgery slot due to this uncertainty. It was like being on hold in the telephone queue. If you put the receiver down, you have to start the whole process again. I was holding out for my *Jerry Springer* moment—'No, you DO NOT have cancer'. Or if that was no longer an option, at least to make the cancer surgery *additional* to the other two. It wasn't like I was bringing another surgeon into the room—two surgeons, three ops, that sounded like a sound investment. I just didn't consider the gravity of which ones were for improving life vs. saving one.

My mobile rang. It was the admissions intake team at the hospital again. I couldn't avoid their call any longer. The adult thing was to answer it and explain the situation. I passed the phone on to Dr Familiar. I needed someone else to speak for me to avoid my potential breakdown.

'Hi, yes, this is Alexandra's doctor. I understand you want to confirm her surgery dates. The thing is, we don't want to cancel the surgery at the moment as we are just awaiting biopsy results for possible breast cancer …Oh I see …'

Dr Familiar started to scribble a phone number on a pad. 'That's very kind of you. I will give her your details and if you can just hold the surgery date for the moment please.'

She turned to me to relay the message. 'The lady from admissions said that she also had breast cancer. She wanted me to give you her number in case you had any questions. She's just returned from being away for a year for treatment.'

A YEAR? I burst into tears. I had only just wrapped my head around possible surgery. *A year* of being sick? How would we survive that? How would I work again? How would I manage the children? A sudden realisation that this would not be as simple as in and out finally dawned on me. I would need to rally the troops, friends and family, but I wasn't sure how and what to ask.

Dr Familiar's face softened as I sat, quietly sobbing. I wanted to avoid having to come back in for the biopsy results. I asked if she could call me with the final results. I didn't want to make a big deal. Just call me, I can process and then wash my face before my appointment with Dr Thorough. Simple.

My request to confirm the results over the phone was denied. Dr Familiar insisted that they could only be given face-to-face. She knew I shouldn't be alone, even if I didn't. I consoled myself that at least it would be another practice run before I saw Dr Thorough. I wanted to be a pageant girl with pre-prepared answers and a fixed smile for then.

'The reception staff will call you as soon as we have them, and you can then come in to see me,' she reassured me. '*BUT*, you are *not* to ask them any probing questions or try to guess the results from their faces,' she said, looking at me sternly. She knew me too well. Another sleepless night.

Friday 27th March 2015

Another day, another call from the doctor's surgery. The results were in. I dropped what I was doing at home and rushed off there. I expected to wait a while and sat in plain view of reception to allow for some more face analysis. For the first time since this all started, I was on my own. Before I had a chance to complete my detective work, I was summoned in.

The doctor handed me a printout of the results and read them to me. I was not sure what the content of this contract would be. The terms and conditions were in invisible ink. Regardless it appeared I had already signed for whatever lay ahead. I was handed a two-prong prognosis, in layman's terms it was bad but not as bad as it could be.

***Invasive* Ductal Carcinoma NST and a High-Grade Ductal Carcinoma *in Situ* and 100% Oestrogen and Progesterone positive (ER+ and PR+).**

I was not sure if it was reassurance that I felt. For what? That my intuition had been right all along? That I had a report in my hands to prove I wasn't a liar, or that Dr Thorough and I would now be on the same page? Over the last two weeks, my emotions swung to an offbeat and erratic metronome. I went from last Friday, *yes cancer*, to Monday, *no cancer*, to Wednesday, *yes cancer*, to Friday, *hell yes cancer!* It was more exhausting than '*The* cancer' and that's saying something.

At this point, you'd think I would just go home and get prepared for my afternoon appointment, but we had some further business to attend to. Besides, what's the shock of having cancer confirmed without a little extra pain as the cherry on top? We needed to address a more pressing matter—the removal of my Mirena IUD. As the results showed, my cancer was positive for Progesterone, Dr Familiar and I both agreed that my Mirena (which releases progesterone) must come out as soon as possible. My body hadn't liked it since it had been placed in six months prior. It was the only thing that had changed in my body since my last mammogram, although no-one can confirm for sure, that this may have accelerated 'feeding' my cancer.

There was another hurdle, Dr Familiar had not removed a Mirena before. My gynaecologist didn't work that day. The only other doctor at the surgery with experience was not available either. I just wanted it out. So, Dr Familiar googled: 'How to get a Mirena out.' Clearly, I'm not the only one who googles! She read the instructions to me.

'Step 1: Contact your doctor.'

'Well, we've already failed that one,' I quipped.

She quietly murmured the other instructions before explaining that she knew what to do. Comforting. 'You'll be my first one!' she said gleefully—double comforting.

So, without further ado, mental preparation, or painkillers, I found myself laid out on the bed, legs ahoy and the old, cool, metal speculum being inserted—or as I lovingly like to call it, 'the metal duck'. And so, began what can only be described as a tug of war. I held my hand over my forehead as if that would relieve any distress or pain. Things were not going well. It appeared to be stuck. I hadn't felt this invaded since my emergency cesarean when everyone was trying to pull a 4.1kg baby back up from my pelvis through to the sunroof. I was beginning to think it would never dislodge and that we would have to leave it there. Then one final yank proved successful.

So excited was my doctor at her handiwork that she came running up to my head to show the Merina to me. Maybe I could muster enthusiasm if it was my children's show and tell, but I was in too much agony to smile. *'Aarrgh*, get the duck out, get the duck out!' I hissed.

My facial expression of 'I've just had my insides ripped out' brought Dr Familiar back to her senses. She promptly retreated to the other end to remove the speculum.

I could finally breathe again and slid my legs back down. I now had one very angry uterus, that was contracting vigorously.

'Quick. I need painkillers,' I hollered. I was beginning to sound like I was in the middle of childbirth.

'Oh sorry, you poor darling. I'll go and get you some from the nurses. I'll leave you to get dressed and meet you at the reception counter.'

I picked up what little dignity I had left off the floor and slowly and cautiously walked down the corridor. I slumped over the counter. Everyone's faces were now filled with concern. I was given painkillers and a glass of water. I could barely look up as I clutched my stomach.

'I'm not even concerned about 'The cancer' at the moment, I just want to stop this throbbing pain,' I added, to no-one in particular.

I gingerly made my way to the car.

6

In Black and White

Friday 27th March 2015

I eased myself into bed. Despite the constant throbbing inside, I was able to rest for a couple of hours. A friend dropped by to hear firsthand the update. I couldn't even get up from my bed to let her in. Luckily, I was close enough to the front door to call out. The ability to welcome people directly from my bed would prove invaluable.

She hurried in and hugged me. I told her the news as if I was talking about someone else. I could see the look of concern on her face. I couldn't think further than this present moment, I was still fixated on my pain. Her eyes filled with tears as the news sunk in. It was the first time that I realised this was not just my journey, it affected everyone around me. She had to leave shortly afterwards for an appointment. It was just as well as there was nothing more either of us could add.

Audrey arrived to collect me for the appointment with Dr Thorough. I somehow managed to make myself presentable. We took our seats in front of the large desk in Dr Thorough's office. I glanced over to check that Audrey had her notepad and pen poised and ready. What if we still missed some information? No time now to employ a court reporter to create verbatim transcripts. Something to ruminate about later.

There was an unnerving and solemn atmosphere in the room this time. His whole demeanour had changed since our last visit. Placed on the table in front of us was an open A4 pamphlet about cancer.

'Louise, did you hear me?' He gently spoke.

I looked back up to see Dr Thorough's furrowed face. **'You have cancer,'** he repeated. Even Dr Thorough could no longer deny the words printed in black and white.

I rehearsed this scene in my head many times. I had the benefit of having a copy of the report for myself (and a couple of sneaky Google moments) so, my response was measured and lacklustre. I had an out of body experience the first time I heard those words, but this time I was ready to launch into the practicalities.

'Yes, but can I *still* have the operation on the 2nd of April, please? ... You see I've got the dogs booked into the kennels, and the children are going to stay at their father's …' I persisted.

If he knew how hard it had been to arrange care for the children the year prior, so that I could fly to England to see my father, he would have understood. Besides, I'd got the dogs placed in kennels—over Easter no less.

'Also, I know that you are only responsible for the hernia surgery, but could you please talk to Dr Practical about still going ahead with the hysterectomy. Then we could do them all at the same time?' I added for good measure.

It's strange what you cling to in the midst of chaos, just to have some semblance of control, even if that means you are asking to have three major surgeries performed together. I would have asked to have a limb removed at the same time if I thought it would convince him to let all the operations go ahead.

'No, Louise. We need to focus on the cancer surgery first. That will inform us of what type and stage of cancer and what treatments are required.'

He pointed back to the open leaflet. He must have a process for delivering news and then talking people through the treatment options using the pamphlet. I was circumnavigating his process and not for the last time.

I obligingly leaned forward to resume looking at the leaflet as he pointed with his biro pen at the different options … mastectomy, lumpectomy, radiotherapy, chemotherapy. It was a twisted menu of options, but I was relieved that he didn't seem too convinced that chemo was on the cards. All these decisions to be made before the surgery. So much to take in, but so much needed to be decided if I was going to keep the original surgery date. I tried to focus on the leaflet and all these new terms, pictures, and information. I'm not sure if my face looked perplexed or disappointed, but he paused.

'I know you're nervous, so I will keep the surgery date open for the 2nd of April.'

That's all I needed to hear. I could now refocus on what he was trying to tell me. Yes, I'll have a lumpectomy. Yes, I'll take the form to book in for the nuclear medicine the day before. Yes, I think I've got it all. I really didn't, but with less than a week to go before the operation, I would agree to *anything* to get this uninvited 'guest' out of my body.

As we left, I felt a rush of relief. If I had to be ill, let's make it a quick one, please. Maybe it wouldn't have to be a year after all. I was so caught up on the surgery date, I hadn't even considered that we didn't know what stage we were dealing with, or if it had travelled. It would be impossible to know what the outcome would be. All I knew was that my scheduled plans for the kennels and children were still good to go. Being able to *relinquish my own timeline* for things and just *focus my energy on the things I could control* would be some of the hardest lessons for me to learn.

For now, I was content. The surgery date had been confirmed. This new paperwork might just fit in my health folder after all. After being dropped home by Audrey, I spent some time with the children before their dad came to collect them for the weekend. I just needed to put my own emotions on pause until they were in his car. When he arrived, I told him it had been confirmed that I had cancer and that I might have to have chemo. He placed his hand on my back awkwardly and before I could even consider this a show of concern he added, 'I have a triathlon race coming up in Germany, will it be over by then?'.

7

Keeping Up Appearances

Waiting for a diagnosis is a bit like waiting for a birth announcement. People buzz around you and want to be part of the action. Living in a small village meant news had spread organically through the mums' network and friends. My Facebook post had alerted friends and family further afield. I had opened Pandora's box of communications but didn't have the resources for individual updates.

'I'll let *you* know as soon as *I* know,' I'd repeat daily.

Most people are genuine, but you occasionally get a few curious onlookers. In the two weeks it took to get the final confirmation, some people started acting as if they were the ones being diagnosed as if it was catching. It played out in the way people would either avoid all contact or remain close with over interest. It was a strange dichotomy to live through. I remember a similar time when my parents announced they were getting divorced. They owned a hotel and restaurant at the time and one of their regulars happened to come into the cafe where I was working. She had just heard the news and was in total disbelief.

'Oh, it's *soooo* very sad. You are *such* a wonderful family,' she said with teary eyes.

I held her hand and mumbled some reassuring words. I told her *we'd all* be fine. I remember thinking her emotional response was very strange. After all, it was *my* family unit breaking down. She seemed to be more invested in the news than even I was. As far as I could tell, the only real impact on her life would be no longer being able to eat at the restaurant. Nevertheless, she needed comforting. It was a role I would continue to play in the months to come.

It was now impossible to shield the children from the reactions of others. It had been especially unsettling for them, with the constant flow of people to and from the house. For a child on the autism spectrum, any changes can cause angst. Seeing my attention turn to others was particularly hard. They already knew *something* was up. Hushed tones and stop-start conversations from visitors had not gone unnoticed. Their little ears would prick up and devour snippets like hawks.

I decided it was time to provide them with an update. To this day neither of them can remember the exact moment I told them. I kept information on a 'need to know basis', short synopses (first time for me!) and focused *only* on the first step. Fortunately, in their minds, I was still going to go in for some surgery on the same day, it was just going to be a different one. Thank God for my pursuit to keep the original date. It meant they both already had time to adjust to the idea of being away from me for two weeks. I admired how adaptable and accepting they were. However, it became very apparent that they would both process the information *very* differently.

Enter Mr Mac strolling casually into the kitchen a couple of hours later. His head hung down and tapping on the calculator of my mobile. 'Mum, you've got a 0.73333% chance of dying,' he nonchalantly announced.

'*What?*' I stopped chopping the carrots for dinner and looked up incredulously. His head still down as if to check the figures.

When Mr Mac was younger, I received an $800 bill shock for a free game called Pet Hotel. I had naively admired what a skilled player he was to acquire so many different animals. When the bill arrived, I realised they were secured through in-app purchases. As a result, I had taken added precautions to hide my phone and update security settings to a level on par with the Pentagon, so I was a little surprised to see him with mine now.

I was accustomed to Mr Mac's more direct line of thinking, but even I was a little taken aback that he seemed so matter-of-fact about calculating my demise. I hadn't even had the operation or confirmation on what my treatment protocol would be yet. I couldn't resist the opportunity to delve deeper into the workings of his mind.

'Umm … how *did* you work that out, darling?' I asked, trying not to sound shrill.

'Well, I took your age and divided it by the population of Australian women with cancer. Then I multiplied it by 1000.'

I was secretly impressed by his logic. Yet a small voice whispered inside, *he really should have multiplied it by 100 to make a true percentage*. I tried to keep my face motionless, fearful that my thoughts might suddenly become vocal. I adopted the 'Short and

Sweet' approach and simply responded, 'Okay,' to avoid prolonging the conversation.

He finally looked up and saw my frozen smile. It appeared to be enough reassurance, and he walked away. That's what I love about him. A deep thinker with amazing views on life. Yet he couldn't always read what is appropriate to ask or catch facial expressions easily.

Adopting silence or just providing simple answers can pacify even his most complex questions. This time was no exception. Mr Mac stores films and conversations verbatim. He holds you to your words like a professional lawyer, so best choose them wisely. Not only would this allow limited wiggle room for further questions, but it would also help me remain emotionally neutral during delivery.

The only other time he asked me another direct question was a few days later.

'Mum … *can I get breast cancer?* You did breastfeed me, didn't you?'

There's that damn logic of his again. My heart ached. How long had he been thinking about this before even asking me?

'No. No, you can't,' I said softly.

In reality, males can develop breast cancer, but this wasn't the time to open that rabbit hole. I didn't want to give him something else to fixate on. I reached over to hug him. It would be one of the few times that I would be able to snatch cuddles as I would be toxic from chemo soon. I would have held on longer if I'd known then.

Then, there was Miss Lipstick. She was a complex mesh of sensitive and silent thinker.

When she was younger, she would clutch my leg so firmly it would appear we were in an awkward three-legged race, maneuvering around the playground. She had an intense stare as a baby as if she was reading your soul. Even the hardiest of Santa's helpers would be flustered at the Christmas photo booth. She would watch things from the sidelines and at times, silently appear in doorways or behind the fridge when you least expected. One time, I was closing the door behind me as I went in to reprimand her brother. I had not realised that, like most siblings, she was behind me to enjoy the show. Her finger got jammed in the door. The bone fractured. She was delighted to recount the story in 'Show and Tell' at school the next day. I prayed that the teachers wouldn't confer as Mr Mac had just made a speech about how even our dog Coco found a boyfriend in the dog park before his mum. We had only just moved into the area. I sounded like a mix of horror mum and loser.

Whenever someone asked her name, Miss Lipstick would look at me for the answer. She would fear making a mistake and would always defer to me about all manner of things, which pencil to use, what she should wear, what she should eat, what she should do. At other times, she would be fiercely independent. She would happily play in her room, organise her toys and lipsticks and often dress like a mini-me. Always the lipstick and make-up, as if she had an urge to grow up fast. It was difficult to anticipate on any one day what way she'd be.

It wouldn't matter if you were a stranger or had met her many times over, she would be hesitant to speak. When she was younger, I would pretend to be finding something in my handbag in the coffee queue. I'd then gently encourage her to place my order for me. I wanted to prove to her (or was it to myself?) that she could use her voice. Then, other times, it would be like a valve had been released. Endless streams of chatter would come out—usually, during the last 10 minutes before bedtime. At first, I thought it was a stalling technique, but really, it was a last-ditch effort to tip all her thoughts out of her head. It was like looking in a mirror.

It came as no surprise then that she would process the diagnosis through a mixture of pictures and questions. Her immediate concerns were more of a practical nature, how would she be getting to and from school? Who would make dinner? What about packed lunches? The subject matter of her questions was a great reprieve from the heavier content of her brother's. Their underlying concern was knowing where Mum would be in all of this. I confirmed that for the majority of the time, I would still be at home. That it would be business as usual. My British stiff upper lip training would serve me well.

The children were a constant reminder of what I would be fighting for. They were a source of inspiration even during my darkest days. Mr Mac's observational commentary on my appearance and general banter kept me laughing and afloat. Miss Lipstick's heartfelt pictures and notes were the cheer squad that spurred me on. They were the litmus test for how we were all doing. As long as I could keep up appearances and still act like a functioning mother, all would be well in their world.

8

The Cavalry Arrives

Monday 30th March 2015

It was a few days before the surgery. The week started with yet another trip to the doctor. Small welts had suddenly come out to play in the middle of my breast. It appeared even my boobs weren't coping. Dr Familiar suggested a 'wait and see approach'. I couldn't risk a potential delay to the surgery date now that everyone was on board. Surely, they would go down in a few days anyway. Or if not, I'd keep my surgery gown on so tightly they'd only be discovered on the operating table. For now, my boobs were in the hands of the gods. Unfortunately, being single, they hadn't been much in the hands of anyone else in recent times. What a waste.

A breast care nurse from a cancer charity foundation called to organise a time to come to the house to introduce herself. Their role is to provide support and information to individuals and their families going through breast cancer treatment. It was a free service and activated by someone unknown behind the scenes. There was so much support, it is virtually impossible to thank everyone personally.

I was not ready to vocalise the full weight of my fears, but this was the first time I began to express a little of how I was really feeling. I stuck to practical questions like, what are you supposed to pack in your hospital bag? I have a habit of packing too much at the best of times. It was suggested I wear pyjamas with buttons on the top for easy access to bandages. It reminded me of packing the same for my maternity hospital bag. My hospital bag then had been prepared weeks in advance. Happier times. Don't go there Louise, you'll just start thinking about not being with the children again.

I focused on manageable tasks to avoid unnecessary emotions—a character trait I had mastered from an early age. I'd learnt to suppress my emotions to suit the room and would silently express them through journals or out of earshot. They were my dirty secret. The general consensus growing up appeared to view emotions as unsightly commodities. I strived to avoid their appearance.

Instead, I acted as if I was preparing to go away on holiday. Much more palatable. I applied a professional mindset to create a 'handover document' for my absence. This ensured that anyone stepping in to help could maintain business as usual. I duly typed up a booklet of information with contact details for friends and family to refer to. It was a checklist of the children's schedules, upcoming school events, the dogs' schedule, and even when the bins needed to go out. I even provided some tips on how to handle the children in my absence and an impressive spreadsheet of my passwords. If I couldn't control what was about to happen to me, then by God, I would have organised paperwork.

I'd chuckled when my mother cleaned her house before the cleaner came. Yet here I was, cleaning ours within an inch of its life. We were open house inspection ready. Even the tiles behind the

The Cavalry Arrives

bread-bin were sparkling. God forbid my life look a shamble to an outsider. I justified this time as a productive use of energy. Besides, my eldest sister was coming. I must show that I had it all under control. Better wipe down the toilet seat again.

I had been in constant contact with my family as I jumped through all the diagnostic hoops. They were searching for ways to help from afar. As soon as my surgery date had been confirmed, my eldest sister, Nicola, booked her flight to come over. She had lived with her family for many years on my side of the world but was now living in England. This would be a more gruelling trip over. The travel time would reduce the time she would be with us to just eight days. I was so grateful that she exchanged her planned family holiday to be with us. She would be a familiar sight for the children. Nicola would be picked up from the airport by her friend and arrive late the night before the operation. I was instructed to go to bed early and she would just slip in quietly.

My other sister Ann was waiting in the wings for the surgery results to be delivered and ready to come over to help with the navigation and selection of treatment options. My mother had wanted to come over in the early stages, but I asked her to delay. I would need to spread out my resources over the year ahead. So much was still unknown, and this was going to be a marathon—one step at a time. Our family may have been spread out in all corners of the globe, but I knew we would all move mountains to be there if the call was sent out.

This wasn't the first time my sisters had turned their worlds' upside down to be there for me. They came over to help with Mr Mac's birth 11 years prior. It had all been carefully planned. Ann would fly in from her home in South Africa the day I was due. She would be there for the arrival of our little prince or princess (we didn't know which). Nicola, living in Japan at the time, would then arrive and there would be a one-day cross over. It would be the first time in eight years, that all three sisters were together in the same country. We'd drink champagne. I would be relaxed and happy with a sleeping baby in the bassinet at my side. Someone didn't get the memo though. Someone was 10 days late and born while Ann was on a return plane home. Complications at birth and possible infection resulted in his transfer to ICU for several days. We finally left the hospital the day before Nicola had to fly back to her own young family. I was determined this time it would be different.

I had also been blessed with a swelling of support from friends based in Australia. A friend from Bondi coordinated offers of support and ensured I had one main point of contact. She kept everyone informed via one call, not ten. A shipment of food was delivered regularly by the Bondi mums. Not only did it contain an abundance of meals for the freezer, but also food for the children's packed lunches. The Bowral mums were a tremendous support system too. Organising some lunches from the school canteen and dropping off treats like chocolate brownies at my front door. It made each step that much sweeter! I was blown away by all the kindness from these beautiful tribes of women taking the reins before and after my family could be there.

A 'welcome pack' arrived a day before the surgery from another breast cancer charity organisation. I'd now become an instant member of the breast cancer community without ever actively signing up. The package contained a box of glossy booklets and even a padded insert to place in your bra. The insert was the most confronting. It appeared even larger than my own boob. How much were they planning on taking out?

The Cavalry Arrives

I always had a complex relationship with my boobs. I was a late bloomer and flat-chested for years. When I did develop tight little buds, I would excitedly display them with pride. I felt I was finally becoming a woman. However, when changing for a gym class at high school one day, I was spotted wearing my starter bra. I was teased mercilessly. I didn't really need to wear one just yet, but I didn't want to be left behind by my peers. At home that night, I remember my father coming into my bedroom to ask me what was wrong. I was mortified, how could I tell him if I couldn't even tell my sisters. I would always remember the name of my tormentor. Ironically, she probably wouldn't even remember mine.

Of course, I eventually caught up. Pregnancy grew them further, but I found breastfeeding difficult. I wrestled with mothers' guilt when I had to supplement feeds. Mr Mac had been taken into intensive care within 24 hours of being born and so we started on the backfoot. I suffered postnatal depression after his traumatic birth and remember feeling such shame when I took out a bottle of formula at an early mothering group. I felt like I had smuggled a bottle of gin into an AA meeting. No-one was necessarily judging me, but I was judging me. I was putting myself under immense pressure to be the perfect mother.

My relationship with my boobs took a more positive turn later when I realised that the advantage of them remaining large, was that they made tops drape away from my body and hide my mummy paunch.

Yes, these puppies and I had come a long way, cysts and all.

9

Game of Knives

Wednesday 1st April 2015

The countdown had officially begun. In less than 24 hours, my body would change shape, literally. It was April Fools' Day, without the prank.

I had not thought much further on my decision to opt for a lumpectomy since my last meeting with Dr Thorough. As a chronic overthinker, I was not sure if this was a new avoidance technique or just incidental. There was no time to wallow, the dogs needed to go to the vets for flea treatment. It was all glamour here. One final call from the hospital and I had my admission time and knew when to start fasting. The spare bed was made. Everything was ready for my elder sister's arrival. My hospital bag was not. It appeared I was still holding out for an understudy to take my place.

I had one more place to go before the children returned from school that afternoon. My final pre-op preparation was at the same place I had my initial mammogram. A perverse full circle to where it all began. Here, I would be provided with a tisane of nuclear medicine—an injection—to help guide Dr Thorough the following day. This was not my first toxic date as it happens. The technician and room were familiar as I had my bone scans there the year prior. I got changed and laid down on the bed that slides into the open-ended machine. That was the first time I had looked at my breast since the biopsies. I remained detached. It was not hard to do.

'Just lie still please.'

I appeared to be becoming an expert at an adult version of sleeping lions.

'I'm just going to inject you with this nuclear medication.'

I looked away as the needle was slowly released.

'Well done. Now, I need you to rub your left breast for about five minutes to ensure that the nuclear meds have moved around … It just helps us get a good picture,' she added cheerily. She left me to it and wandered off behind the glass screen.

I cringed at the request but started the circular motions. It was the most excitement I'd had in weeks. It did seem a cruel twist of fate that I would have to bid farewell to my faithful friend. Goodbye left breast and thanks for the mammaries … I mean memories. The jury was still out on how much I would be left with. There was always a chance that I may need a second surgery if Dr Thorough didn't get enough free margins around the excision. Only time would tell if I'd made the right choice. From this point forward, I would need to turn the volume dial down on unsolicited advice from others regarding my treatment choices. I would need to trust and remain faithful to my decision.

It seemed to take forever to put the children to bed that night. When I eventually slid into my own bed, I couldn't shake this restless feeling. The cancer booklets were piled up on the bedside. They taunted me. It felt like I was about to have a major exam and hadn't studied enough. There really wasn't anything else left for me to do but show up.

I kept my bedside light on and anxiously listened for a car to turn into the driveway. From the moment my sister arrived, I felt I could finally take a deep breath. I may not have been able to abandon the ship, but I was certainly ready to let my sister take the rudder. After a quick chat and a cup of tea, her friend departed. We both went to our rooms. We needed to catch what sleep we could. It was going to be a very early start.

Thursday 2nd April 2015

The morning ran in slow motion. I served the children breakfast and tried to keep the atmosphere like any other day. When it came time for them to head out for the bus, I started to wobble. Both my sister and I went to the front door to wave them off. The enormity of the situation suddenly hit me. I began to well up with tears. I tried to still sound cheery as I called out goodbye.

'Hold it together,' my sister gently said beside me.

My smile was strained. They didn't look back. Thoughts fired off in my head. Would this be the last time I saw them? What if something happened in surgery? What if I didn't wake up? My knees started to buckle.

The hospital was in the centre of the village. Although it appeared small, it could handle multiple surgeries and was very efficient. The local staff were kind and caring. By the end of the year, most of them would know me by name, if not by sight. It had free and easy parking—a luxury not available at most hospitals. My sister marvelled at how you could just drive right up to the surgery front entrance. The reception check-in was more resemblant of a hotel than a hospital. I chatted and laughed with the receptionist whilst completing forms. I was acting more like a guest than a patient. My sister teased me for being just like our mother and chatting too much. I teased her back, saying she sounded intolerant just like our father. I enjoyed the banter exchange. These lighter moments helped break any tension. We were given menus to look over and waited to be called. After a nurse repeated the information provided, we were allowed to move into the prep area for surgery. I was handed a gown to change into. We ended up in fits of laughter at the size of the disposable knickers that were provided.

'Good lord, do they get any bigger?' I asked the nurse, while wondering how big she must think my bottom is.

She returned with the largest size they had. It could cover a small car. I suddenly felt good about my body shape.

As our giggling subsided, my thoughts returned to the children. They would be away for two weeks with their father. He lived about an hour and a half away. There would be no chance of any drop-in visits. I told myself that this would be for the best and essential for my recovery. More than that, it would give me some space to process the results of the surgery (type and stage of cancer) and ensure that I resumed a somewhat perky persona for their return. I suddenly felt an urge to see them. I wanted them to see that I was upright after the surgery, so they wouldn't worry whilst away. Or maybe it was for me? Their father was picking them up from school that afternoon so there would be a chance for them to swing by. I made my sister promise to call him. I knew that if she asked, he would listen. My nerves subsided, knowing that I would see them again. I then said goodbye to my sister and was whisked away to the pre-op holding area. Once again, alone with just my thoughts. A dangerous place to be.

Dr Thorough appeared at the door with a big smile on his face.

'How's my *favourite* patient?'

His energy was upbeat and a complete 180 from the week before. It appeared he would be on fire for the surgery. I was looking for any positive signs that day. I shed a couple of tears when the anaesthetist arrived with the happy drugs.

'Please make sure that you don't give me *too* much sedative. I get worried that I might not be able to wake up. Please make sure that the nurses call me Louise, or I won't respond,' I rattled off.

He gave me a pre-med sedative to take the edge off. He probably gave me a double shot to shut me up for all I know. But whatever he gave me, I was grateful for the reprieve from my mind chatter. I gently drifted off to the land of nod.

The next thing I remember was being back up on the ward, in my own room—room number 8. Another good sign, my favourite number. I felt high with relief and the possibilities of living … or maybe that was just the drugs? I was deliriously happy that my 'uninvited visitor' had finally been removed.

My sister delivered on her promise. The children were bought to the hospital. They shyly shuffled into the room one by one, checking out all the tubes. I'd already asked that they be warned that I might look a bit bluish/grey from the dye that gets injected to help locate the sentinel nodes during surgery. If I did look like a Smurf, they didn't tell me. What I didn't know at the time is that this blue dye hangs around your nipple area for a few more days after surgery. Sadly, I wasn't up for going to Coachella to really take advantage of this.

They didn't stay for long, but it was wonderful to see them. That night, I excitedly rang a few friends to tell them the cancer was out. I thought I was effervescent and eloquent on the phone but was later told that I didn't make a whole lot of sense. That night, I would live on cloud nine. The next day, I would come crashing back down to earth.

Friday 3rd April 2015

It was Good Friday. Or as I like to call it, not so Good Friday.

My sister arrived in the room at the same time Dr Thorough was doing his rounds.

'It was much deeper than I thought it would be, so I had to take more out …'

(not a great start)

'You *will* need to have chemo ...'

Wait, *whaat?*

'I've taken some samples. If we don't have clear enough margins, we may need to do a second surgery.'

Oh God, another anxious wait.

His use of a practical tone made all the sentences feel like they had the same weight of importance. In reality, the update felt it was a warped version of the 'feedback sandwich technique'. He'd subtly used 'you'll need chemo' as the meat between two other not so great slices of feedback bread.

I wasn't prepared to hear the word 'chemo' so soon. Tears began to trickle.

10

The Will to Live

My eldest sister was practical, level-headed and the rock that I needed. She was my cook, nurse, and gatekeeper. Friends were vetted, and my sleep times were mandated and obeyed. My electronics were confiscated to limit disturbances. It reminded me of boarding school. I enjoyed the structure and knew she was doing this for my own good. I needed to be in shipshape, not only for the return of the children but for what was still to come.

I had only had a short peek at my breast at the hospital when I asked for the surgical tape to be removed. The tape had been so itchy and had been driving me to distraction. Now at home, I took a longer look. It reminded me of a dent in a car fender. The scar was jagged in a Harry Potter kind of way. I traced it with my fingertips and could feel the scar tissue knitting underneath. My left nipple now pointed sideways. My right one naturally pointed the other way. It was as if neither could bear looking at each other anymore. The scar under my armpit from the removal of the lymph nodes was deeper and more painful. I avoided looking at them again for some time to come.

I felt cabin fever begin to set in. I wanted to go somewhere—anywhere—for a change of scenery. The last few weeks had been a holding pattern. I was a plane circling above my normal life with no clear instructions of what lay ahead or when I could land. I was desperate to join my sister for her daily coffee, but she would go alone. I just wanted to see some life around me, to people watch, even if I couldn't fully partake. I just kept quiet and didn't press the point. I used the time to scroll through Facebook to confirm that the world was indeed still turning. Looking back, I guess it was her time to process and regroup.

After the Easter weekend, I needed to get the rest of my 'house' in order—that is my will. I had been so focused on preparing for surgery that now that the dust had settled, I had to think of what would come next. So, I asked my sister if she would be the executor of my will. It was not an out-of-place request as she was already the executor of my father's will. I didn't consider if she even wanted to or what the role entailed. I just pressed ahead. It needed to be completed in just a few days so that she would still be in the country to sign. Well, that is what I told myself.

A friend who is a lawyer generously offered her services as a gift to our family. She conducted the meeting with such compassion, ease, and grace. It was the first time I had spoken of the true nature of our financial position. I had hidden the extent of our debt, even to the family. 'We're all fine,' was the party line.

The reality was I had to take a lot of time off to take my son to therapies. I tried to negotiate this with employers, but you begin to feel more like a liability than a team player at work. I couldn't fully explain to my family what was happening at home. I didn't want to admit I was not coping. My earning capacity fell as I reduced days to try an alternative way to manage all the appointments. These were a requirement outside of the normal parenting scope of children's illness or school holidays. Drop off at school started to require another teacher to prise Mr. Mac's fingers from clutching at my clothes. I would start the onward journey to work with tears in my eyes as I heard his cries for me not to leave. I was on an out-of-control hamster wheel. I was either constantly trying to catch up at work when I was late in or rushing back to pick the children up from after-school care on time. I had no ability to outsource and routinely felt I wasn't being enough to anyone.

However, I had an unwavering belief that the more input and help Mr Mac received early on, the easier life would be for him in the long run. I wouldn't have had it any other way. As we had missed the majority of funding for early intervention, we were now set on a financial trajectory that I couldn't stem. I had to access my superannuation (pension) early, sell some gold jewellery, including my 21st birthday present—a great grandmother's watch. It didn't touch the sides. We moved away from Sydney's high rental costs which eased some of the burden. I was so grateful that we could also access medical and community support programs that we'd otherwise not have been able to afford. An added bonus was that the children would experience living in a rural area, as I had in my childhood.

I had underestimated the amount of stress I had been under daily during this time. I had been living in fear and hypervigilance for so long. The slightest deviation from a carefully planned schedule to provide our family with stability would spin me into overwhelm. Life had become a game of chess. I was spending too much energy predicting every chess piece move. I'd lost the ability to focus on making one move at a time as I tried to strategise my way to the end of the game. I wanted a guaranteed end result. I was drained and unable to remove myself from the board. This chronic stress had a major impact on my own health and the reason we were now in this predicament. Living in a constant 'what-if' scenario wasn't healthy. If I lived through this, then I knew I would need to find a better way forward. For now, though, I just needed to get through this meeting and divulge my financial situation in front of my sister.

'Let's start with your assets, Louise,' the lawyer began.

I was glad I was not facing my sister as I could already feel shame begin to rise. It was the part of my annual tax return that I would dread the most. We could always fly through this section. 'Yes, it's the same as last year … no shares, no house, no other additional income,' I would repeat on cue.

This time, I would need to think about what I could say for at least a few lines to be on the document.

'Ummm … my assets?' Nice Louise, stall for time. 'Ummm … I have some jewellery—mainly beads, the furniture of course … Oooh and some lamps … Oh the two dogs … and of course the children!' I chuckled. Pitiful.

'Okay, and what about liabilities?'

'Umm liabilities?'

Apart from the way I handle money? I wondered.

'… Well, there is the car … I'm still paying that off for a few more years. Then, there are some credit cards … how many you ask?

Oh, a few … umm,' I felt uncomfortable and hot under the collar. I dared not glance sideways as I could feel my face flushing.

The lawyer carefully reviewed her notes.

'So, it's about $30,000 in total?'

Oh God. I looked down. I'm not sure if I had ever added them up. If you keep them separate, then it doesn't seem so bad, does it? I didn't even know the figure. I cringed. A survival mindset means you have to deal with the hand you have and can't let thoughts take you too far into the future. Cancer was making me face the decisions I had made to help me understand what had led me to this point. I was tired of validating my choices to everyone, including myself.

'To clarify, if Nicola is my executor ...' I paused, thinking about how I could put it delicately.

'Will *she* be held responsible for my debts?' I added half-jokingly. I feared the colour would be draining from her face as I spoke, so I avoided all eye contact.

My pension life insurance would clear any debts but that would leave the children with less. Financially things would be rosier if I was no longer here. Not really the carrot to encourage you to live is it?

Another name was put down for a trustworthy friend to also be permitted to access my bank accounts. Best to keep the cone of shame wide-reaching then. This would also mean she could make any necessary arrangements in lieu of my family.

Discussing my financial fragility bristled. I was so stooped in shame that I couldn't see how much I *had* achieved. I was living in terms that to be successful in life, one should be financially affluent or solvent at the bare minimum. It was an unfair yardstick. My first thoughts awaiting my cancer diagnosis did not ever yield regrets at not earning more. I had a sense of peace with the memories made with the children, the dogs and our family life. If the time I had spent with my children and focusing on their development were always my raison d'etre, then why could I not look at that as my success? Only when I allowed myself to tune into my heart would I know that to be true.

Tears endlessly flowed when we talked about arrangements for the children and the dogs. I was given space to unravel and time to collect my thoughts. Discussions turned to what was legally possible and what my ideal would be. I knew that if I was no longer alive, my sisters would remain steadfast in my children's lives and ensure that I would not be forgotten. Nicola had the most remarkable way of quietly facilitating and organising the most magical milestones in life without wanting recognition for her efforts. It couldn't have been easy for her to hear me talk about final arrangements. I'm not sure if I would have been able to be so strong if it was the other way around.

By the time we left, I was emotionally spent. Looking at my demise full-frontal took the wind out of my sails. If I could look beyond my death, then surely getting the surgery histology would be easier. Confronting as this day had been, I came away with a sense of relief I'd faced shame and fear head-on. Their grip had been released slightly. Although I had no legal control of how the children would be raised, being able to express my wishes and have them heard somehow unburdened me. Knowing that my wishes would still be represented even if I was gone, provided some additional peace.

The Will to Live

I was due to get my results from the breast surgery from Dr Thorough the same day my sister had arranged for a family friend to visit for lunch. I knew a copy was also being sent to Dr Familiar. The temptation was too much. As soon as I knew the results had been delivered, I called to make an appointment with Dr Familiar. She wasn't available. They wouldn't release the report without me seeing a doctor. I didn't care which doctor; I just wanted the printout. After all, I was a professional doctor by then.

We all know by now that prior preparation prevents my anxiety performance in front of specialists, but my sister did not. The appointment would be just before lunch. I was prepared to drive myself, but she insisted I not go alone. She rang to delay our guest's arrival. I could tell she was irritated that I intended to circumnavigate the process. I don't think she could understand why I would not wait a day for Dr Thorough to provide them.

The not knowing for me was way more stressful. I needed to know if I should expect death. Firstly, I would then have an extra 24 hours to live my way. Secondly, I would be better placed to not fall apart in front of Dr Thorough. I'm not sure which of those were more important to me. Now, where were the notepad and pen? Looking back, this was really the first time I stood up for myself and voiced my needs to my sister or any other member of my family. The six years age difference had always created the natural big sister/little sister relationship. Even as adults, I would revert to that dynamic. I finally started to express what I wanted to do rather than follow what others expected. For years I had felt like the odd one out in the family, school and some friendship groups. Now, I was beginning to realise that although my way of thinking and being might not be cookie-cutter, I had the right to pave my own way and create a full life on my own terms.

Another report and more big words.

'20mm invasive ductal Carcinoma cancer, Grade 2, margins clear. Moderate nuclear grade ductal carcinoma in-situ, margins clear.'

I didn't spend a long time with the doctor. I went through the motions to appease the report release etiquette. I wanted to get a copy of the report, go home and google. Our guest arrived when I'd only had a chance to skim through the full report. The size of cancer removed was smaller than originally reported. I imagined that a Dyson-style extraction of the cancer cells before surgery had been the upside of having two biopsies. I was later told that wasn't the case as the original reports were just estimates. The conversation flowed at lunch and focused on the news that the report had stated that the first operation had achieved clear margins. I wouldn't need a second surgery and the sentinel nodes 1–3 were negative, so no travel there. My breast markers (what was feeding my cancer) were 90% Oestrogen positive and 100% Progesterone. I was fortunate as this would open up more options available for treatment than some other types of breast cancers.

I glanced back down at the paperwork as the conversation changed tack.

'I wonder what "Vascular Invasion" means?' I interrupted. I knew that the word 'invasion' didn't sound like a polite guest.

'*You've got* to celebrate the wins,' my sister admonished.

11

50 Shades of Chemo

There was a week between Nicola returning to England and Ann arriving from South Africa for a fortnight. The children were still with their father, so I had one precious week alone. I began to read the treatment information booklets. I tried to approach it as if it were a research project for a client. Who knew that there were over 50 shades of chemo available (actually more like 100) and that one size does not fit all? In fact, your treatment plan is so tailored to your individual needs, that it is impossible to compare and contrast. All you can do is read through generic treatment information. The Rubik's cube of different combinations is the domain of your oncologist.

How do you know what the right version is for you? This new world was so alien to anything known to me and included a bewildering list of stats and medical terms. All you can do is listen to the advice from the specialists, do your own research and make an informed decision in line with your own personal circumstances. Then just follow your treatment protocol and release expectations and control of the outcome. Take one step at a time and adjust the treatment course as required.

The gap between the operation and starting chemo was only a few weeks. Enough for the healing from the surgery to start, but hopefully not enough time for the cancer to have spread. I now needed to meet my oncologist. I was so fortunate that the oncology department was at the local hospital on the ground floor. It took me several failed attempts to just walk down the corridor to make an appointment. Once I stepped through those automatic doors, there would be no going back. I just wanted it all to stop. I've done surgery before, but chemo? My only reference was what I'd seen in movies like *Terms of Endearment, Love Story* and *Beaches* and it didn't look good. Can't it just all end with the surgery? I finally reached reception many U-turns later. I needed to familiarise myself before the real appointment in a few days. Or maybe it was easier to role-play the part of chemo patient than admit I was one?

Since I was down a sister, another friend came with me for my first appointment with the oncologist. He was an experienced specialist and director of two cancer centres in the area. He was a softly spoken and mild-mannered man. His room was functional and serene, which helped quell my anxiety and focus on the discussions at hand. The breast cancer nurse also attended to capture the information. He continued to calmly explain treatment options based on my surgery results. He was unflustered by my incessant questions and need for a visual timeline of treatment. I referred to him as Dr Calm for that very reason. From what I could gather, it would be like preparing for battle. Surgery was the first phase of attack. Chemo eliminates the chance of enemy lines being broken and further invasion. Radiotherapy is the local mop-up of stray soldiers. Adjacent hormone therapy (in the form of medication) is the peacekeeper that stays on the ground for a few years until everything is stabilised.

It was also the first time that I heard I was in the grey area for treatment options. I was hoping for a direct order of action. I didn't want to be the only one responsible for this onerous decision. There was a lifeline ... you just had to pay for it. A test called the **Oncotype DX Genomic Test** had just become available in the last four years. I was an ideal candidate. The test uses a sample taken from breast surgery to analyse how the cancer is likely to behave and respond to treatment. This can help doctors more clearly understand the risk of cancer coming back and if there is a benefit to having chemotherapy after breast cancer surgery. A sample would need to be sent to the USA for analysis (there were no laboratories in Australia running the test at the time). Yes please, where do I sign up? Finally, this could be my lucky day! Just one last thing. The test cost $4,500 AUD and wasn't covered by Medicare or private health insurance in Australia. It was, however, covered by Medicare in the USA and by the NHS in the UK. Memories of the recent discussions over my will came flooding back. This would not be an option financially. I was too afraid to ask for help.

I arranged to see a second oncologist. I didn't want to second guess myself. Maybe they would magically make all this go away. Perchance there was a new vitamin I could take instead? At the very least, they would provide me with some reassurance that I was on the right path. Ann would arrive just in time for us to go to the appointment together. Nothing like a bit of pressure decision-making.

Ann was the sister you would call to break you out of jail. I would regularly visit her abroad for unbridled fun and to let my hair down. I would spend a lot of the time laughing and whipping her children into a frenzy. There's nothing more joyful than being the crazy aunty. Ann was a great sounding board for matters of the heart. She would ask my boyfriends the awkward questions I was afraid to. I'd act coy as if I was shocked that she'd asked, but secretly was glad. She was my confidante and guide when I separated from the children's father and helped me through that difficult time. Now that I was living so far away, we hadn't really spent as much time together. Ann had only met my children a couple of times over the years. They were much younger then. I was looking forward to her coming over, but I would be less carefree, and the stakes were much higher this time. Laughter would not flow as freely.

The second specialist was based in Sydney. We would need to make a round trip journey. As we arrived at the plush offices of the new specialist, my legs decided to make a hasty dash back to the lifts.

'Come on, what are you doing?' my sister asked quizzically. She was probably wondering why after we'd been happily chatting about the appointment in the car for a couple of hours, I was acting more runaway bride than curious patient.

'Just *give* me a minute,' I pleaded.

I retreated to the chair opposite the lifts and around the corner from reception. I was beginning to hyperventilate. What if the news was bad? What if he said I had no choice? What if … what if … Well, we would never know if I didn't make it through that bloody door. Time for those big girl panties.

The second oncologist explained the conundrum with the test at that time was, although it could indicate yes or no to chemotherapy, there was a wide area in between for the 'we don't know what you should do'. I knew that with my present standards of luck, that would be exactly where my bullseye would hit. So, I asked him the same question that I'd asked at my other appointment.

'If I was your daughter or wife and you didn't know that this new test was available, what would you be advising?'

'Chemo,' he said without hesitating. Both oncologists did.

I had spoken earlier to a friend's husband who'd been an oncology nurse. He provided an insider's point of view. He told me that the hardest part of his job had been seeing patients with a returned cancer left wondering 'what if' they had completed more treatment in the first place. I also knew that I would have to look at my own unique set of circumstances. I needed to give myself the best chance at survival to see my children grow up. If I had to play Russian Roulette, then I wanted to put extra bullets in the chamber. I felt now I'd covered all my bases.

When I returned, I called the local oncologist. I asked to start chemo as soon as possible so that my sister could attend before she had to fly home. This meant that there would be no time to get a chemo port device surgically implanted into my chest. Ports eliminate the need for needles. The device allows chemotherapy medications to be delivered directly into larger veins and is easier for drawing blood samples. Instead, I chose to have all transfusions via a cannula into my smaller network of veins. My left arm was now effectively redundant since surgery and the removal of some of my lymph nodes under my armpit. It is recommended that the arm is no longer used to draw blood from or for blood pressure tests to limit the risk of lymphedema and arm swelling.

At the time I didn't understand the regularity of blood samples required. They were an integral part of analysing levels before and after chemo treatments and for general wellbeing checks. This meant that my right arm would need to be used for *everything*. I didn't really think that through at the time or what the consequence of my choice would be. Somehow, I was more focused on delivering a unique experience for my sister as I felt she'd been cheated from seeing my son's birth last time. Had I known the issues further down the line to get a cannula in the wonky veins of my right arm for the next few months and beyond, I would have probably delayed starting. You don't always know what you don't know.

The first few days, Ann helped create some order around the home. My ability to keep on top of things had taken a nosedive. It appears things were beginning to pile up both inside me and the house. It was a relief to have help to get us back on track—Marie Kondo meet your predecessor, Ann. She arranged for a handyman to come in and fix shelves in the laundry area so that things were within easy reach. Found a place to hang the mugs next to the kettle in the kitchen, making it easier for visiting guests to help themselves. This newfound order was a welcome elixir to this extended period of chaos. It kept me preoccupied and feeling a sense of accomplishment. On the outside, it would probably not have been on everyone's priority list, but we had been raised to be houseproud. Afterall, I was going to be in this safe container called home for many weeks to come. It was the practical help that I needed, which can often be the most overlooked. The peace and joy it provided—priceless.

If I was already feeling the strain of being out of my routine, the children were not far behind. My checklist had not anticipated what to do if we weren't coping. The days the children were at school were filled with household projects and additional medical appointments. The night-time was spent kid wrangling. Time was being eaten up. I'm sure our family unit would have looked very different than what Ann was used to. Or anyone else for that matter. She had four grown-up children of her own and had ample experience with children, just not with mine. It's a tough gig looking after someone else's children, even when everything is calm. It would be a more extreme sports activity at this time.

The lead up to my first chemotherapy hung heavy in the air. I tried to play the perfect host and mother and released any anxiety with ill-placed humour. I asked my sister if something happened to me, could she bury me in a wedding dress. I'd never been a bride. It might be my last chance to wear the outfit. To talk and joke about the dark, taboo and inappropriate was our family's way of coping in difficult times. Or maybe just me?

The next day we were late for my orientation appointment at the oncology centre. I was hurriedly trying to put on some mascara while navigating the lawn in front of the entrance.

'You won't need to use that soon!' my sister remarked.

I promptly burst into tears. I knew she was trying to lighten the mood. I just hadn't considered losing my eyelashes or eyebrows till then. I logically understood that I would lose the hair on my head. I didn't realise that you lose the hair in your ears (that can affect your balance and hearing) or in your nose (which makes you more prone to infections). On the plus side, not having to shave my underarms or legs for several months would be a nice bonus! By the time we reached the cancer centre, I had composed myself.

For a place that shelters such dark times, it is a remarkably uplifting and hopeful haven. The staff were always incredibly welcoming, compassionate and supportive. We were somehow all in this together. The underlining theme was to keep upbeat and not make something difficult even more challenging. Why do we have to wait until a crisis to learn this? The day unit, where the administration of chemotherapy takes place, is the beating heart of the centre. The room is filled with individual treatment bays and large comfortable chairs around the edges. Pictures hanging on the walls prevent it from looking too clinical.

The induction meeting took place in a separate office adjacent to the room. It was the first time I had met the nurse unit manager—Nurse Nurture—or anyone from the oncology unit itself. The first thing I noticed was her warm smile and friendly blue eyes. She could read my thoughts and emotions before I could. She provided bite-sized information for me to digest. The induction was a marathon session of things to expect—the good, the bad and the ugly—well I would discover that for myself later. They say the devil is in the detail, but micro-detail is like Xanax to my anxiety.

It was also a chance to uncover what potential weak spots might flare up when my immunity was low. My main area likely to be tested was my chest. I tended to get asthma or chest infections when my immunity was low. This would prove to catch me out several times during treatment. The one gift I thought chemo might give me was a slight body of a twenty-year-old again—alas, I would end up being so pumped with steroids I would look like Vayrs from *Game of Thrones*. The session ended. My head was spinning. Thank God my sister was there to capture the long, drawn-out list of medication and supplements for us to buy. A local charity was able to help cover some of the costs. A welcome subsidy as the cost of the incidentals was adding up. Anti-nausea, steroids, anti-anxiety tablets, were just the three I would have to take before I'd even stepped back into the cancer centre for my first chemo. Nurse

Nurture held space for me as I tentatively raised my questions. I was beginning to get good at this. I felt both seen and heard.

Having someone live with us full time was proving difficult for the children. We had been in survival mode for so long as a tight-knit family of three, that the changing dynamics was hard for them. Tensions were rising. My sister was trying to restore some structure in the household within the limited time she was staying. In return, the children were demonstrating escalating behaviours. Their lapse of manners, not eating at the table for more than five minutes or appreciating the food she had cooked was glaringly on display. We were on the verge of a mutiny. I had lost the captaincy of this ship.

The reality was, the children had already seen me through diagnosis and surgery, but the sound of chemotherapy sounded a much scarier prospect. I didn't have all the answers they needed at this time. This accumulated in further acting out, elongated bedtimes, bedwetting and endless washing. Everyone was clawing for my attention. Ann would retreat into the garage to have a sneaky cigarette and escape the children or me or both. She didn't want them to know she smoked. However, they knew exactly where and what she was doing. I would plead with them to not let on that they knew. I didn't want to hurt her feelings. I felt like a referee as everyone would confide in me what they were finding difficult. I was beginning to look forward to escaping for chemo!

The night before my first chemo, a friend and her children came over and provided a much-needed diversion and some banter. Dinner was eaten without complaint and everyone remained seated at the table—a small win at last. This allowed me to return to preparing for the next day. A side effect of one of the chemo drugs was sensitivity to light. This can cause the nails to fall out. I was directed by Nurse Nurture to paint my nails with black polish the night before treatment to effectively block the light. My friend painted my nails before they left. It was one less thing to do myself. I was deeply touched by the gesture.

I was pleasantly surprised that the antidote to the fallout from chemo could look *soo* fashion-forward.

12

Treatment Treadmill

The pieces were now falling into place. I had a diagnosis. I had surgery results. Now I would be starting on what I called the 'Treatment Treadmill'. Head down and keep stepping forward. Unlike the gym version, there were no buttons to speed things up. Steep inclines were included along the way. All you can do is hold on to the bars, not deviate from the treatment plan and keep your eyes on the prize. Assume the worst and hope for the best, to avoid disappointment. I hadn't yet factored in that I should also have my own desire to stay alive.

Wednesday 29th April 2015

The day of my first chemotherapy session arrived. It had been meticulously planned out. Haircut at 8:30 am, chemo started at 10:30 am and back home by 3:30 pm in time for the children returning from school.

Nevertheless, everything came to a head. We reached code red before the first item on the agenda. It was only 8:00 am.

I had started my morning packing a bag to take with me. I was wondering what the clothing etiquette for chemo was—J-Lo Velour tracksuit? Hamptons weekend-wear? Or just the trusty BIG W store tracksuit and top? I heard voices gradually rising from the kitchen.

A showdown between my nine-year-old and my sister was taking place. If memory serves me correctly, it was over what to eat for breakfast. To be fair to my sister, this wasn't the first time Miss Lipstick had broken an adult. Our first au-pair disintegrated two weeks into her tenure. 'Jasmine doesn't like me,' she bleated. 'Jasmine doesn't like me at times too, and I'm her mother,' I responded. So, not the first altercation I've intervened, but just not today, please.

My sister appeared in my bedroom doorway.

'I can't deal with your children,' she snapped, threw her hands up in despair and walked away.

I sighed and stopped what I was doing. I just wanted to walk out the door and leave them all to it. I left my room to round up the children and to tell them all to pull it together. One look at their faces, I instantly knew what I had to do. They wouldn't get the bus today. I couldn't do it to them, or to my sister.

'Quickly, grab your school bags and get in the car.'

I marched to the car and diverted my trip to the hair salon. Like a judge, I heard all their protests in the car to school. I had no energy to battle with them or confront my sister right now. I just reassured them that I would be home by the time they came off the bus. I lovingly waved goodbye from the car and screeched around the corner to the hairdressers. I didn't want to be late, especially as my hairdresser had opened early for me.

I returned home to collect my sister but did not utter a word about the events of the morning. Filed that under 'don't go there'. I have a dossier of those. We arrived at the hospital with my bag, pillow, and latest blood results. Internally, I was a bundle of nerves and had all the signs of a cardiac arrest. On the outside, I was a duck above water. So thankful that we had finally made it to the centre.

The padded recliner chairs in the oncology centre reminded me of airline business class seats—with stool lifts for added comfort. I was led to my station and placed my bags down. There are unwritten rules about chemo treatment—a sort of patient etiquette. A healthy respect for each other's space, privacy and ability to have treatment in peace, entwined with an overriding sense of fellowship. I rearranged my bags and proceeded to unload items I might need within reach as if we were about to take off. I had been in such a rush to pack, I wasn't sure what I had with me. It appeared that I had everything and then some. I had several books, magazines, and even a small tapestry. I hadn't completed one of those since I was about twelve. Those visions of Victorian ladies had inspired me. If I couldn't beat them, I might as well sew with them.

I lay back into the chair and the nurse strapped me up to the blood pressure monitor. Just as she started taking my temperature through my ear, I suddenly felt something shoved into my mouth. It was a digital thermometer from home that my sister had thrust in when my gaze was averted.

Like a pilot, she was doing her final safety checks that the instruments were operational. After all, the first night would be on her watch. I looked up and saw concern flashing across her face. I was worried that the mix of sleep deprivation and events spinning out of control weighed heavily on her. We were all just hanging on really. It was the first time I really saw the strain the situation was having on her. It's not easy playing the carer role. You are doomed if you do something and feel doomed if you don't do anything at all.

The initial checks concluded my blood pressure was going through the roof. A visiting therapy dog was brought in and carefully placed on my lap. I wished there were two. I'd called a friend from the hairdressers to download the family stand-off from earlier. She'd unexpectedly arrived at the centre to show her support. I just wasn't sure how this would be received as we continued to tiptoe around earlier events. The nurses asked my friend to wait until my first bag of fluids had been started. It was the perfect time to also suggest my sister go get herself a coffee. I needed to recalibrate after such a bumpy start to the day.

My friend was then ushered in. The volunteers offered her a plunge coffee. I felt dreadful that I'd just sent my sister off to find her own. I didn't know that was even an option. When my sister returned, she sat awkwardly next to my friend. I could tell she felt like a third wheel. I tried to engage them both to have a conversation, but it didn't seem to make a difference.

I was grateful to be interrupted by two nurses. They approached at a befitting solemn pace, dressed in lilac disposable gowns and plastic gloves. One was pushing a metal stand with the first bag of chemo dangling down. The bag was covered in a black sleeve. This was the light-sensitive one. It matched everyone's mood. Whilst my cannula was being hooked up, the other nurse came forward with a pair of cold therapy gloves. The inside of the glove was filled with a gel substance that would freeze like a cold pack and slowly thaw once worn. They were designed to ease the side effects and prevent the nail from lifting off the nail bed. I'd known that I would need to wear some frozen gloves during one of the intravenous infusions of chemotherapy. I had not envisioned that they would be more oven mitt in structure than a fitted glove. I felt ridiculous for having packed needlepoint. I would not only be unable to pick up things wearing them, but my cannula tubes would also make it near impossible to even flex my wrist.

Some oncology units also offer frozen caps to try and prevent your hair from falling out. This was not an available option at my cancer centre at that time. I'm not sure if I could have withstood both. I was already feeling more like Scott from Antarctica with frostbite. With both treatments together, I fear I would have looked less like Elsa from *Frozen* and more like Manny the mammoth from *Ice Age*. The frozen gloves and caps and black nails are no longer offered for treatment due to updated research on their effectiveness. Seems I may have been overdressed for treatment after all. I'm glad I covered all the bases, nonetheless.

My stats continued to drop, resulting in the chemo to be literally drip-fed through. I had not accounted for my body resisting treatment in this way. I had naively assumed that everything would run like clockwork. It was agonisingly slow and clear that I would be a prisoner of this chair for way longer than expected. My last words to the children suddenly came to the fore. I'd told them not to worry and that I would be back at home by the time they came off the bus. I wasn't sure everybody would have had enough time to forgive and forget this morning's fiasco. I needed to make sure that my sister was prepared and could cope with the incoming balls of tired and emotional children as I feared they would take my absence as a bad sign and be worried.

There was little my sister could do sitting here with me. I thought I could persuade her to go home to catch some sleep. Nana naps had been my go-to tool over the last few months and helped me cope. Perhaps they could work for her?

'It's going be a while. Why don't you just go home and sleep?' I suggested quietly.

I'm not sure if she took this as an abrupt dismissal, but I intended to help.

'I'm not going to go and *sleep*,' she sounded irritated at the suggestion. 'Although, I could use the time to go and get some things organised?' she added on further reflection.

'Why don't you bring the children in after they get off the bus?' I added casually. 'By that time, I will have had my second bag of chemo and my last saline flush bag will be in. That way, they can visit the room where it's all happening … The nurses said it would be quieter by then too,' I suggested, in an attempt to keep their time together more manageable.

She hesitated. Then gathered some of the excess items I no longer needed and returned home. My friend stayed a little longer until my eyelids began to droop. The poison was now surging through my system. I had not a drop of pretence left. I eventually dozed off. This chemo malarky sure was tiring.

Later in the afternoon, Ann returned with the children. They looked wary as they surveyed the room and empty chairs. Miss Lipstick clutched at her baby doll. It had a Tic Tac stuck in its mouth. One of the nurses noticed and asked her if she would like her to 'operate' with some tweezers and get it out. She silently followed. Mr Mac looked up and down at the cannula and mentally noted that it all looked similar to the last hospital. He then started to look restless and kept asking when we could go home. To my surprise, everyone seemed calm. Maybe I overreacted that morning? I hoped by seeing the room any unspoken fears the children had would be eased. I was so grateful for all the care from the nurses and volunteers that day. They really are all unsung heroes and went above and beyond by fussing over the children and making it all seem very normal.

Finally, we returned home just before 5 pm. The hardest 9–5 working day I've ever had. I lay wearily on my bed. Miss Lipstick snuck through the door. She was desperate to show me a book that the school counsellor had given her that day. It was about cancer. I was a bit taken aback at the detailed information it contained. It looked like it was for a child beyond her years. I realised they were trying to help, but even I hadn't been given that much detail. Fortunately, she had been enthralled by the cards you could cut out and show your friends. They said, 'Don't talk to me. My mum's got <insert type> cancer'. Oh God, I could just imagine her in the playground. In retrospect communication tools like these might have been useful for me.

We had just started to flip through the book together when my sister burst through the door. Miss Lipstick quickly retreated.

'Come on. You've got to get up from your bed. You've got to show them that you're fine,' she scolded.

I pulled myself up and sat at the table.

I'm not sure whose benefit this was for more.

TREATMENT TREADMILL

Pre-diagnosis
February, 2015

Post-Breast
Cancer Surgery
April, 2015

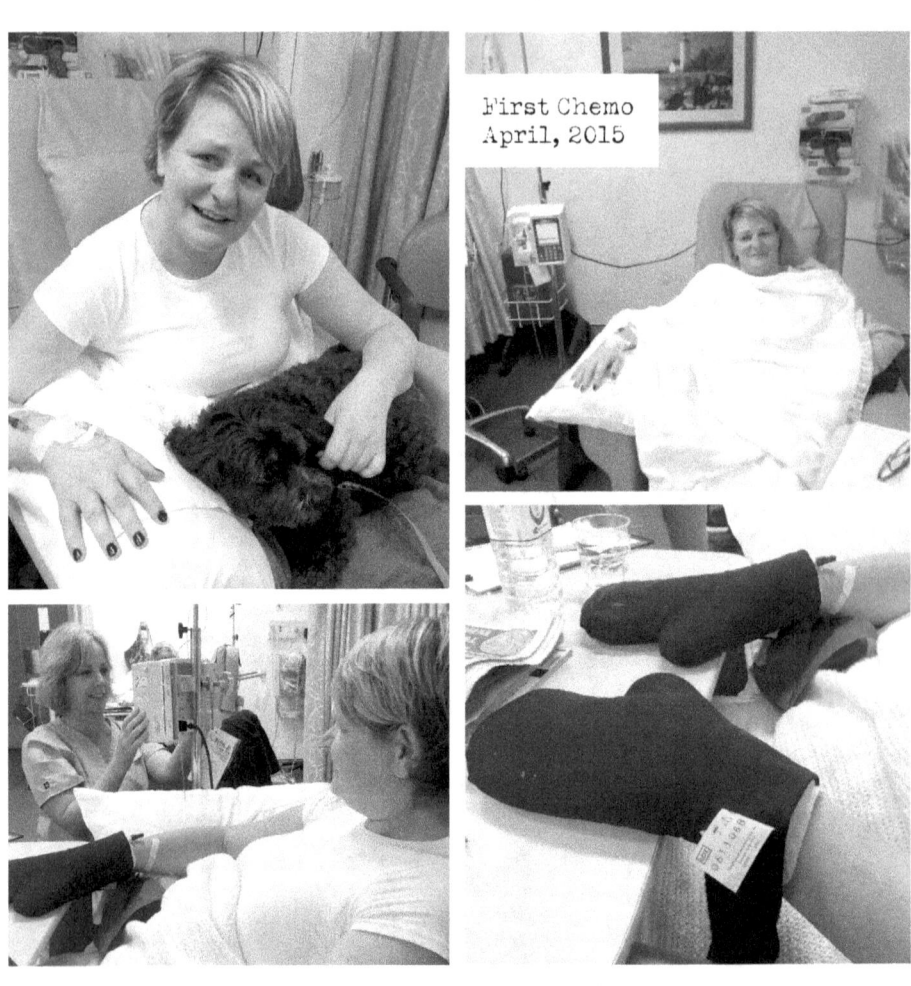

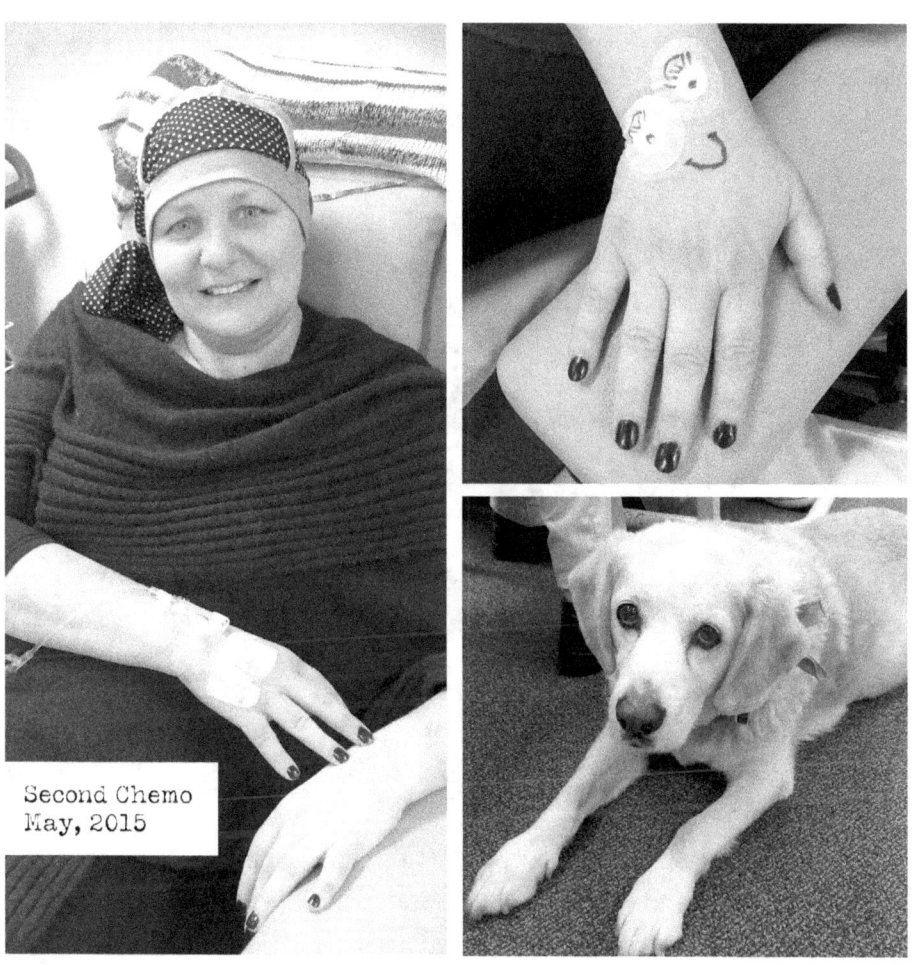

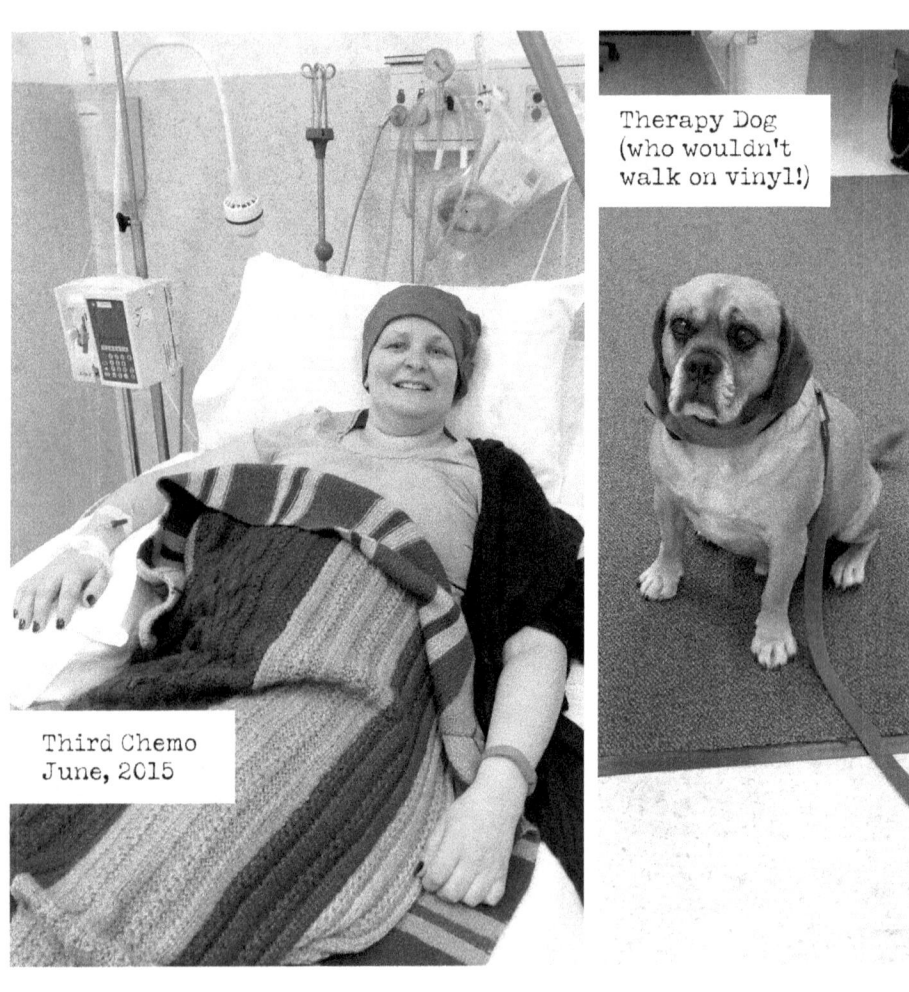

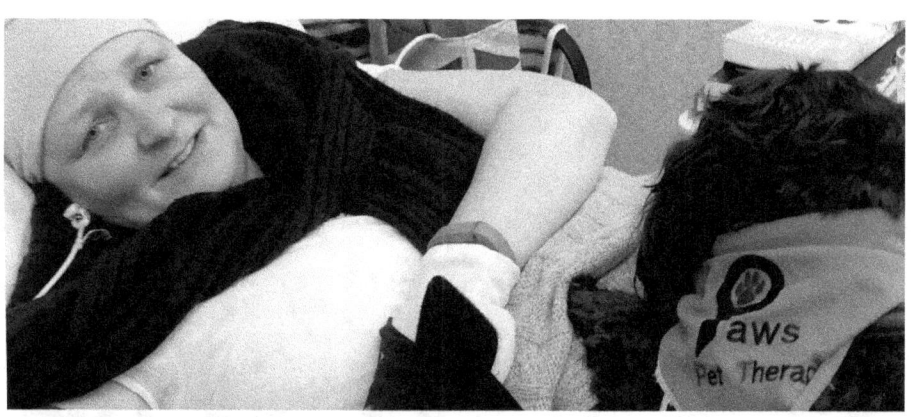
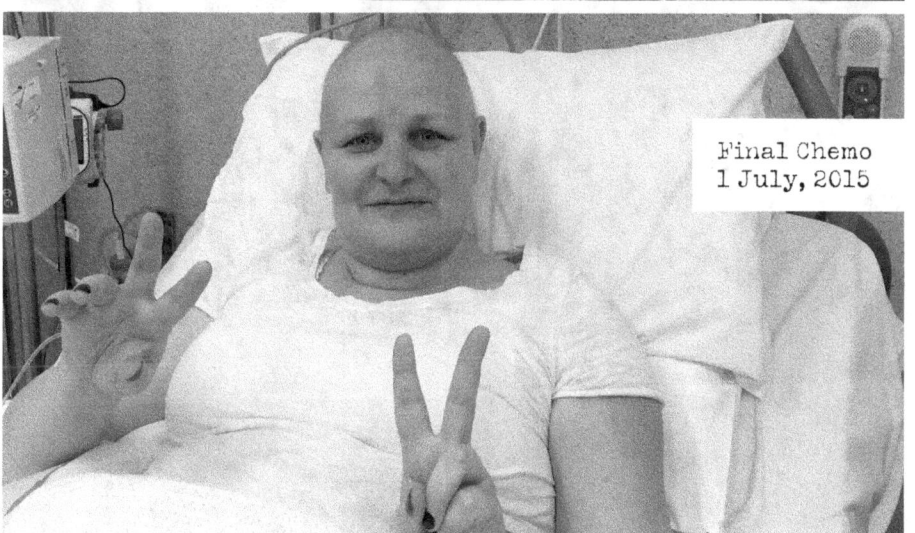

Final Chemo
1 July, 2015

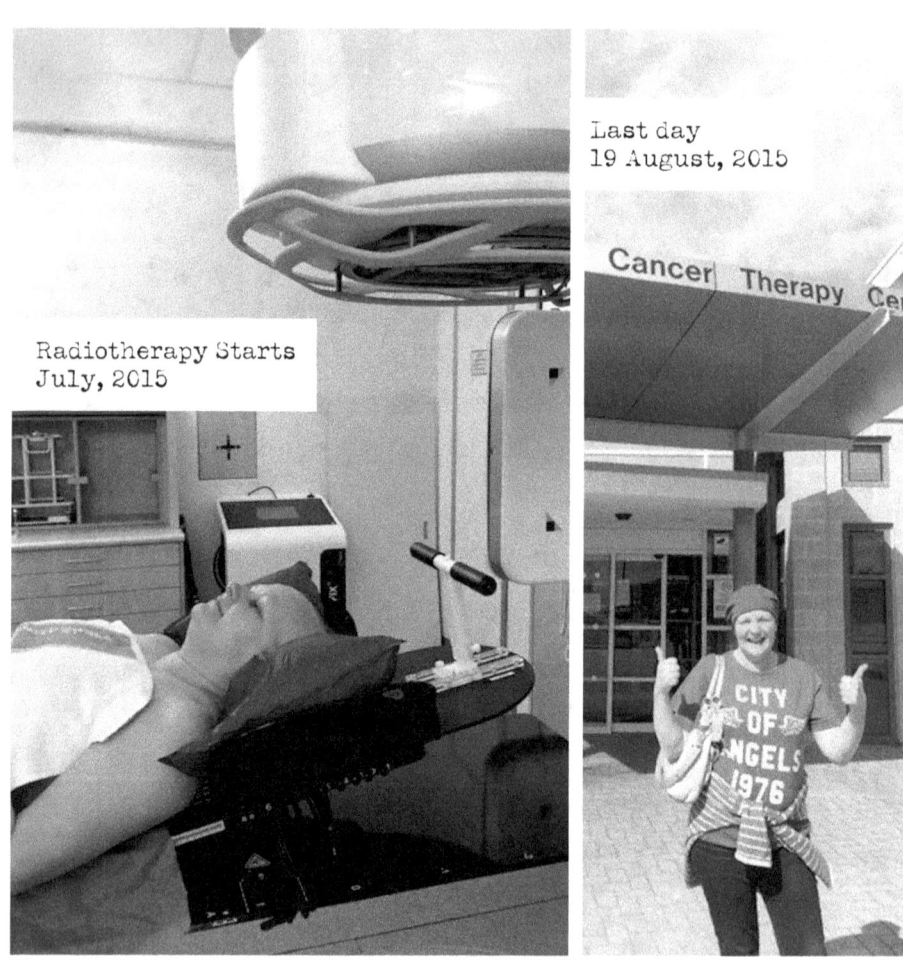

ALL THINGS BALD AND BEAUTIFUL

Hair Shaving Day
14 May, 2015

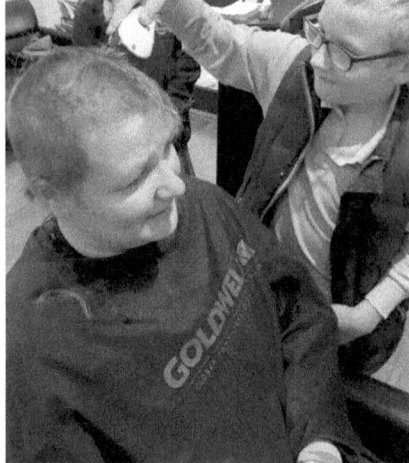

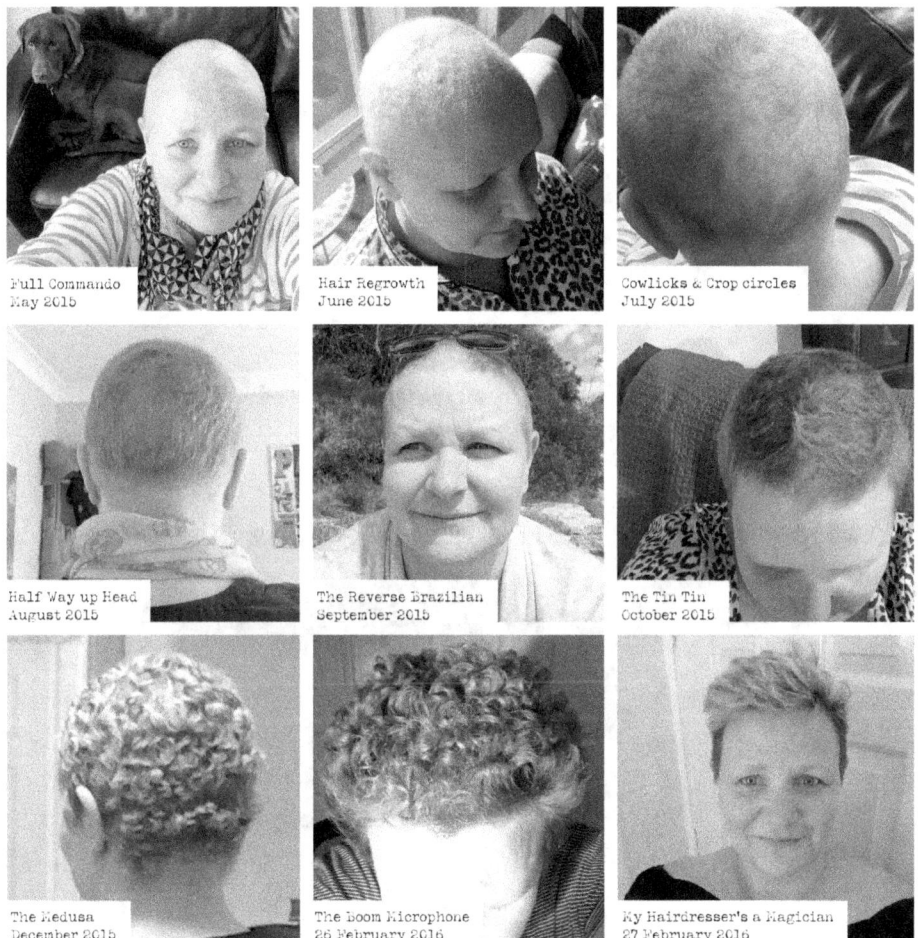

MISS LIPSTICKS NOTES OF INSPIRATION

Mother's Day card
10 May, 2015

I will never forget you
14 May, 2015

Whispering Girls
June, 2015

my mum has a twinkle in her eyes when the sun hits her eyes I havent seen a single time when she dosen't have that beautiful big long smile on her face, her tears are like lemon drops and hardly come out of their sock her little baby hair and head shine in the dark and her eyes are as blue as the sky (on a sunny day at lest) I love her if she was a animal she whould be a beautiful dove with sparkly wings

Baby Hair
July, 2015

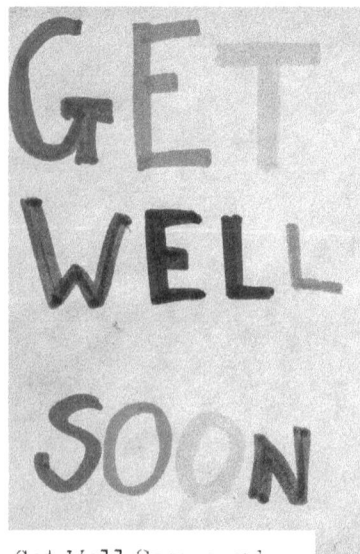

Get Well Soon card
10 August, 2015

Cheer squad Notes
September, 2015

#mum is great, awesome, beauitfy, loveing, helpful, my favourite parent, funny/ridiculas and much much more

#don't change anything about you! you are perfect in every single way PS: rember! don't you dare change! ☺ # love you mum

Dear mum,

I love you with all my heart and even though it can get rough sometimes just remember I'll alsoways love you. you're so many things to me mum, best friend, FPITW, Guradian, helper, carrer, dancer, singer and much much more

I ♡ U

13

Cause and Effect

The dogs were reluctant to come near me that first night. It was as if they could smell the poison. I was relieved when they were back by my side the following day. The first few days after chemotherapy, you are like a toxic pariah. You have to use a different shower and toilet from everyone—thankfully, our house then had two. You also have to avoid handling food in those early days. My sister had flown home a couple of days after the first round of chemo so I would now need to more heavily rely on friends. I'd spent so many years being self-sufficient. I was usually the caretaker, so asking for help did not come naturally. I would need to break that barrier. As I got sicker, I would have no choice but to surrender. A friend of mine helped me see reason. She said that if the tables were turned, I would have helped in a heartbeat. It was just now my turn.

The children appeared to grow up overnight. They stopped sneaking into my bed, so I guess being toxic did have some benefits. They became more self-sufficient. Perhaps driven by my need for them to help themselves on days I struggled, or a desire to know, if something happened to me, they'd be okay. My role was to stick to the treatment program. I'd never been so laser-focused or determined.

I just needed to look upright at the beginning and end of each day. I could collapse into bed in between. No-one would be the wiser. It was the first time I started to listen to what my body needed. I was still struggling to find work and was getting frustrated. I felt like a student again, with a generous amount of free time between terms, but no money to go anywhere.

After my first round of chemo, I felt surprisingly well. I proudly presented my blood work report to the oncologist, expecting a gold star for my efforts.

'Oh, it *wasn't* as baaad as I thought it would be!' I said gleefully.

'Well Louise, that's *not* what your blood work tells me,' he looked at me pitifully.

Damn, I forgot to google. Reading blood work was not my forte … yet.

'Your white blood cells have all been but obliterated. You will now need an injection after each round of chemo to help your body make more white blood cells. Look, you can see here on the report if you don't believe me,' he gestured.

I'd secretly hoped that this one-page report of numbers, would show that I was the anomaly patient. I would be written about in medical journals. I hadn't considered that it was very early days to be so confident. The last time my optimistic outlook had been this crushed was when I was breastfeeding with a grazed nipple. Not so bad the first time, but then gradually getting more painful with little time to heal in between feeds. Then, and now, there was no option but to push through.

Cause and Effect

I felt I might have jinxed myself when a few days after my first chemo, I had a sudden urgency to go to the toilet. A sudden gush and the bowl was crimson. My body started to shudder. Thankfully the children were at school when it happened. I thought if I took action immediately, I could 'fix' myself quickly without them or anyone else, even knowing. It was the first time I realised how quickly things could go downhill. I was petrified that this was something sinister and immediately drove to the cancer centre. Blood was taken as soon as I arrived to establish what was happening. I tried to calm myself by thinking it might just be a heavy period. A last hurrah to my endometriosis. It turned out to be a side effect of the chemotherapy, irritating the bladder lining. It was the volume and speed of the bleeding that had me shaken.

It appears I now had issues with white *and* red blood cells. I'd always fantasised that I was a person of noble birth with blue blood. I was ready to let that dream go now. I couldn't cope with more. And yet, it appeared that I could and would. So, let's just give a quick run-down of some of the effects I had that weren't necessarily written in the brochure...

The injection to stimulate 'healthy' white blood cells in the bone marrow makes you feel like you've aged a hundred years.

You can suffer from dry mouth and ulcers, so you will need to use a gentle mousse toothpaste. Your tongue will have a metallic taste to it as if wrapped in aluminium foil.

That fatigue you felt before? Well, triple that.

Your appetite will be of a limited range, mainly baked potatoes, and chicken soup. That's if you can muster an appetite.

Your eyesight will change, and you'll get dry eyes that require frequent drops.

Your hearing changes, balance shifts, you are way more susceptible to any infections (especially tricky if you have petri dish kids coming back and forth from school).

There will be temperature spikes, and my own personal favourite, explosive, burning stools as toxins leave the body.

Nausea waves, nausea waves, and did I mention, nausea waves??

CHEMOPAUSE. Yes, it really is a thing. The chemical effect from chemo is a wrecking ball to your body. It literally slams you into a state of menopause with hot flushes galore. Like mothers who discovered that children's 'witching hour' is not limited to just one hour, these flushes would appear from nowhere, anywhere, and at any time. Not great for your self-esteem. On the upside, being hairless your hot flush would run up and out of your crown in no time. Best to pack a fan in your handbag, nevertheless.

Chemo treatment undulates like the sea. The first night after the poison has been absorbed, you are being crushed by a giant wave. The first week after chemo, you are caught in a rip-tide and struggling to keep your head above the water.

Week two after chemo, you notice the shoreline and feel some hope that you can reach it. Another wave carries you towards the beach and spits you out, bedraggled and coughing up salty seawater. You are a mess, but you are alive.

Cause and Effect

The third week after chemo you dry and dust yourself off and take a moment to breathe. You sit on the shoreline with your face towards the sun and your toes cooling in the water. Once settled, you'll realise the tide is coming back in. It's time for your next treatment. Back to sea you go, just that little wearier than the last time.

I would find several ways to counter the effects. I would try to befriend my insomnia and nausea. I would distract myself with British comedy clips, *Saturday Night Live* sketches and standup comedian sets on YouTube. Short bursts of comedy were all my brain could manage. Laughter would replenish my soul. I would also try to spend as much time as possible in nature. I would take snapshots of the seasonal changes to remind me that life goes on. I tried to make it feel more like a staycation then a confinement. Somedays I could venture no farther than our garden. Other days, I might make it up the street. I would just have to remind myself that any step forward may require a step back. I paced myself rather than force strides from my home safety net. The children would still need to be taken to appointments. Short car trips into town to pick up forgotten items from online shopping orders. Fortunate really, as otherwise, I might have become agoraphobic.

I would reluctantly attempt to remain quiet and still. I wasn't good at that yet. I would write and connect on Facebook with friends from the confines of my home. I would look to find joy and laughter within each day. But most of all, I would try to be present with the children and savour their laughter and our collective giggles. We were back to being our tight-knit unit of three once more and muddling through the last terms of the school year. The daily ins and outs of school life kept me grounded. I began to receive cards and notes with inspiring messages from Miss Lipstick. These kept my spirits up in ways she could not have fathomed.

Two upcoming high school interviews for Mr Mac were a welcome diversion and fell between rounds of chemo. I had no idea how much joy the interviews would provide and how much I'd swell with pride. They supplied the fuel to see a potential future where I would see both my children reach high school and beyond. I was grateful that my hair, barely clinging on, was still there for the interviews. I wanted to avoid embarrassment for him, for them and maybe for myself too.

The first interview took place just a week after my initial round of chemo. It was for a small non-denominational school that his father had suggested. It would rely on Mr Mac securing a scholarship. I was not keen on this added pressure, especially at a time where he was already dealing with so much.

It was as if Mr Mac could read my mind, 'If I don't get the sponsorship, I won't go. It's too expensive, I want you to concentrate on getting yourself better and not to worry,' he lovingly added. He always was more mature than his years.

His father would come down from Sydney to also attend the interview, which I knew would make an already nervous Mr Mac more anxious. I just told him to be himself.

'Do you like playing sports, Mr Mac?' asked the admissions officer.

'Yes, yes I do,' he cautiously responded.

I couldn't look at him as I knew this response was more for the benefit of his father, an avid sportsman.

'Do you play on any teams?

'No.'

'What sports do you like?'

'*ALL* of them?' His replied.

'Do you have any hobbies?'

He looked across at me as if lost on how to answer. I gently placed my hand on his knee under the table. 'Perhaps you can talk about your writing?' I suggested. It was enough of a prompt to get him back on track.

'Yes. I'm on my third book' he replied.

I smiled. He had easily moved from lost for words to an academic scholar. I had recently been shown a collection of stories by his teacher. I wasn't sure I'd call it a 'book' exactly, but I loved hearing his confidence. He was now on a roll.

'And what would you like to be when you grow up?'

'A biologist, a zoologist, a medic…'

I thought he was stopping but he continued.

'I'd like my legacy to be like Einstein … and when I'm older, I would like to be a soldier and protect my country.'

I caught the eyes of the admissions lady to see her look of acknowledgement at this extraordinary soul. I was so glad to have just let him be true to himself, unfiltered, unedited, and magnificent.

Not only had he covered all career bases, but it would also rival the worlds' best beauty pageant speech.

We were interrupted by the principal coming in. The admissions lady provided him with a quick summary: 'This is Mr Mac; he is on his third novel and would like his legacy to be like Einstein.'

A great summary indeed.

After such a revealing interview, I was intrigued by how he could possibly top that. It was just a week later that his second interview for a larger catholic school approached. We were interviewed by the head of drama, so I thought if nothing else, she would find him a great orator. I was never sure where his mind would go, but I hoped that his anxiety had now lessened.

'Have you ever been bullied, Mr Mac?' she asked.

I could feel my heart quicken. Please don't mention school camp. Please don't mention school camp, I repeated in my head.

'Yes,' he paused and then replied, 'Thirty-three times.'

I wanted to reach out and hug him. Had he really kept count?

'What subject do you *not* like?'

'Scripture.' He answered without missing a beat.

At least I could never be accused of prepping his answers.

14

All Things Bald and Beautiful

I was invited to attend a 'Look Good, Feel Better' workshop at the cancer centre, an initiative by the beauty industry. It provided products, tips and tricks to help ladies going through cancer feel confident in their appearance during treatment and beyond. I wasn't much of a make-up girl, but it was so wonderful to be invited. It was a chance to meet other women going through this journey. The room was filled with love and a sense of camaraderie that day.

We were all at different stages of treatment, some with hair and some without. I became a little self-conscious as I tried on the various headgear options laid out on the table. I never knew there was such a range of options and things to consider—block colour suits a wider range of clothes, but patterns can make a statement. I'd imagined that I'd suit the Elizabeth Taylor turban look. Turns out I looked like Hilda Ogden from the British soap, *Coronation Street*. Best stick to beanies then. We learnt how to put on make-up and were generously given a bagful of goodies to take home. It was lovely to attend a more uplifting event after the seriousness of the other appointments. That night, I went online to panic buy some headwear—one in black for the night and one in red for the day.

The children's reaction to my new short hair had been priceless. They focused their attention on how 'ugly' it looked rather than how I'd just had my first round of chemo. I took that as another win. It was a short-lived one. A couple of weeks later, I was shampooing my hair in the shower when it started to come away. The day before, I had enjoyed having some wind through my hair. I wished that I could go back in time. I cried as I saw the clumps falling through my fingers and down into the drain. I carefully patted the rest of my hair dry, desperately looking in the mirror to see if it was obvious. Just in case, I wore a hat that night for Mr Mac's next interview.

I used to have long hair when I was younger. One day, I decided that I wanted to cut it into a bob. My mother tried to dissuade me, but I was adamant. She relented on one condition. I would have to pay for the haircut with my own pocket money. If after a month I still liked the haircut, she would pay me the money back. I decided it was a fair deal. When the hairdresser made the first cut, I knew I had made a huge mistake. I remained poker-faced with a bottleneck of emotions for the rest of the appointment. I thanked my hairdresser and quietly left the salon. I cried all the way home. By the time I was near our house, I had wiped away my tears to prevent any signs of regret. I considered it better to cover up my disappointment and get my money back then admit my mistake. My stoic resignation of difficult situations had been ingrained early on.

To further add to the pain of losing my hair, just two months earlier, I had proudly bought a GHD hair straightener. I'd imagined all the parties I would be going to, looking stylish and fabulous. Now it would be gathering dust. There was only one option left to me now. Take back some control and shave it. So, I booked an appointment for the day after Mr Mac's final interview. Once again, my beautiful hairdresser opened the salon early so that we could visit before school. I thought we would face this part together as a family. The advantage of before school was it would then allow me time to process alone. I hadn't even considered that it would not just be myself that needed that time.

We were the only ones in the salon. Each child was given the clippers to help shave some of the hair off. The mood wasn't as upbeat as a charity shave off, but enough that Mr Mac was so enthralled using the clippers that I had to check that the safety latch was on. Miss Lipstick took her turn. She only wanted to do it once. I should have known then. All I could see in the mirror was the tiniest of hair stumps protruding, dark circles from sleepless nights and my reddened eyes as I held back my tears. It was the first time I had really seen how sick I looked. What I didn't see was how disconnected I was from my body and my emotions back then. It would take me a few more years to truly be myself again.

I dropped the children at school. They silently left the car. I sobbed all the way home. I remember sliding down the wall of my bedroom and releasing a primal cry. I held that position for an hour. Dark thoughts crashing over me. What if I was not here to buy Miss Lipstick's first bra? Or when she has her first period? Or gets married? How will Mr Mac be able to transition to high school? Who will help him cope with the changes? I might not see them grow up. Heavy-hearted, these random thoughts swilled around my head on a repeat cycle. Eventually, I could wallow no longer. I guess another silver lining from chemo—dry eyes. You can't cry a lot.

The hairdresser had taken pictures so we could mark the occasion. It wasn't until later when I scrolled through them that I saw it was a hollow victory. Miss Lipstick's eyes were devoid of their usual sparkle. She had emotionally retreated. I thought that it would bring us all closer. I had underestimated the profound effect it would have on her, on us all. That night, Miss Lipstick came into my room and shyly presented me with a picture she'd made. It was adorned with inspiring and positive messages around the edges including **'Don't listen to everyone else,' 'Floow <follow> your dreams,' 'Be humrus <humorous>,'** and **'Be yourself.'** My heart melted. She admitted that she was worried I'd be teased for not having any hair. I thanked her for being so brave and for helping me shave my head even when it was so hard for her. Before I could beat myself up too much about involving her in the shave, I had to suck in my cheeks to suppress a laugh. I noted that my beautiful daughter had ended with the words *'I will never forget you!'* I wasn't sure if she knew something that I didn't.

Little known fact. Short stumps of hair actually hurt, as they fall out a bit like a painful ingrown hair. A friend did some research and discovered a silk pillow would be softer on my head. I discovered that when sweating out toxins from chemo, they evaporate quickly when you have no hair—another silver lining. My buzz cut stumps started to drop out in sporadic patches. I didn't quite get the memo that if you are wanted that smooth peach look, you need to shave off the rest with a razor. Instead, I looked like a hedgehog that had been caught in a lawnmower.

After #clippergate, Mr Mac declared, 'I can't take these many changes. I've only just got used to the last change!'

'I preferred you with shorter hair,' Miss Lipstick quietly admitted.

Yes, that'd be right. You all now prefer the hairstyle that you'd previously called ugly! We've got a long way to go still, so buckle up everyone.

I began to wonder how Parisian women with chemo navigated these times. They were always incredibly stylish, but I wasn't smart enough to search on Instagram. Besides, at that moment, my desire to look polished was minimal. It was winter where we lived, so comfort and warmth were my priorities. Who knew that bald heads got so cold? Beanies were my staple. I was so grateful for the friend who knitted me some. I laughed though, when a well-meaning friend sent over a package of scarves. They had skulls and crossbones on them. Fashionable? Yes. Match my inappropriate sense of humour? Yes. Nevertheless, I was cognisant; it was not something tasteful to be wearing around other patients undergoing treatment at the cancer centre. It appears I might have a filter after all. My make-up supplies from the Look Good, Feel Better event, lounged in their bag. I knew I'd make use of them eventually, but for now, I'd probably sweat them off before I got out the front door.

I avoided mirrors at all costs. I knew enough from the pity look on people's faces. My chubby face from the steroids along with my bald head would be confronting for anyone. I was told later that it was my dead-looking eyes that were more of the giveaway. So, to defuse anyone from feeling uncomfortable, I would be upfront and say what we all knew but didn't want to say—I looked terrible. It's like when someone has an ugly baby, and everyone is struggling to find something good to say. When everyone remarks, 'Oh look at the baby's lovely fingers,' you know your baby is ugly.

I knew everyone was sympathetic, but I decided to be my own spoiler alert. To be brave and real. Well, as brave as someone who still couldn't look at themselves for long in the mirror could be.

I did try alternatives to the classic beanie/scarf. I tried wearing a wig. There was a wig library at the cancer centre. At first, I balked, fearing that these might be second hand. Not sure if it is a thing. The lady who ran the program was so friendly and compassionate. She could see I was hesitant. I glanced at the shelves for options. I was a bit overwrought.

'What about the Raquel Welch?' She proffered, reaching for the box.

Oh God, they have names? I politely looked over, but inside was panicking.

Of course, this is the time that you could go all out and choose something outrageous and different. I could tell from Miss Lipstick's drawings that she was trying to get her head around me wearing beanies. One of her pencil drawings contained a street scene including me wearing a hat, scarf and T-shirt with a '**for brest <breast> cancer**' slogan on the front. I was being admired by Ramdun (random) girls on the street whispering '**She looks beautiful**' and '**that looks good**'. It was her gorgeous way of making me feel special. I would regularly be depicted with a beanie, which she'd noted as '**Classic**' Mum. She just wanted her mum to look like her mum. My beanie had now become an acceptable part of the norm. I wasn't sure if a further change might tip Mr Mac over the edge, but I also wanted to feel a bit more feminine. After much laughter and trying on a few more, we settled on one that looked remarkably like the short haircut I'd just had—the new me as it were. I would take it.

They tell you that wigs tend to have 20% extra hair in them so that you can cut and style them to suit. I was feeling buoyant at having an additional choice of headwear. I wanted to blend in more. I made an appointment to go back to my trusty hairdresser for help styling it.

It was one of my favourite memories. We both danced around the awkward fact that there really wasn't anything that could be done with this particular wig. It appeared to neither have much additional hair to be cut or options for styling. My hairdresser played around with it for a while. We caught each other's glances in the mirror and she tried not to look discouraged. I could tell that we were at the end of the road when she tried to slide in some ordinary bobby pins (Kirby grips) to make a difference.

Rather than voice our disappointment, we both oohed and aahed politely to make each other feel like we'd found a solution. We laugh about it now and how long we prolonged the agony. Eventually, I left the salon in one of those 'don't worry, I'll wear it out' movie moments. When I got home, I realised that the rubbish wheelie bins needed to be put out for collection. As I dragged them up the driveway, a massive gust of wind came out of nowhere. The wig unattached itself and sat like a toupee at the top of my head.

The next day, I returned the wig.

15

Cancer, Models Own

A week after the head shave, it was time for my second round of chemo. I was beginning to find my treatment rhythm. The day before, blood tests were taken to confirm I was alive enough to take the poison. The day after chemo, I would return to have my white cell injection. There were so many needles I felt more pincushion than human. My veins seemed to be constricting and shying away. It took three attempts to get both the vein and cannula to work together. As the poison was finally released, I felt a sharp sting. I stayed seated and silent. The alarm from the machine alerted the nurses that we still had not struck vein gold. The tell-tale bruises across my hand the next day illustrated it had been a rough start. Note to self, there are no prizes for remaining in agony. I was advised next time to wrap a warm towel around my arm and hand before coming in. This would make for friendlier veins. I needed to be friendlier to myself too.

Another full day in the chair for treatment. A friend accompanied me for part of it. I left the needlepoint behind. The following days blurred into a mix of nausea and toxicity. There are so many levels of tiredness with cancer treatment. You do something physical like make a bed, then lie down. Clear out the fireplace, then lie down. Make a cup of tea and then lie down. My daily mantra became … Surrender to the pain, the weight gain, and retiring to your bed at multiple points in the day.

We were so blessed with financial and emotional support pouring in not only from my family but friends and even strangers. I had finally reached out to my own family to ask for help to keep a roof over our heads. Our landlord delayed selling the house so that we could have some stability during treatment. I was humbled by the generosity and unsolicited assistance from people. Friends raised funds with a morning tea and auction, another group organised a collection to help pay for a cleaner, more food deliveries, chicken soup batches, books, DVDs, chocolate brownies and even a box of wine to help me celebrate small victories along the way. We were nominated for the 'Highlands Sisterhood Dinner Drive' a local charity initiative that provided a box of items for dinner, some toys for the children, and a magazine for me. People picked up the children to go on playdates to allow them some reprieve from being surrounded by sickness for a couple of hours. This helped break up the monotony. Cards and letters from friends were like little sparkles of light along the way. All this practical help allowed me to keep my head down on the treatment treadmill and combat the debilitating exhaustion of it all. I continued posting on Facebook little moments along the way to feel connected. I felt wrapped in a blanket of unconditional love and care.

As my body became more war-torn my resolve became a little wobblier. I had underestimated the emotional toll. I had been hopeful of securing some freelance work and even dressed up, beanie and all, for meetings. I'd stayed up late to prepare a proposal for one potential client. It took me twice as long as it would normally. I had come to expect that now. My mind had become more fuddled. I couldn't remember simple passwords (thank goodness for that magnificent spreadsheet I'd prepared earlier). I'd sent the email off just in time for my next chemo session.

My mobile rang. I quietly took the call. I was hoping for some good news.

'Hi Louise, have you got time to talk?'

'Well ... as I mentioned in the email, I'm actually just in the middle of treatment at the moment.'

'Great!'

Is it really? Or had she just not heard what I'd said?

'Well, we loved what you've put together, but we realise we just aren't ready for the next steps quite yet,' she continued.

'Oh. I understand,' I replied, trying not to sound too despondent.

'Well, speak to you soon!' she ended cheerily.

I sat, staring down at the phone. Poison continued to drip into my veins. That night, I would take another call from the family.

'Have you got a job yet?'

'No,' I said deflated. They wouldn't know how ill-timed the question was.

It was as if Coco, our chocolate Labrador, could feel my anxiety. She would position herself at the top of my bed in close proximity to my head. I would often wake up to find her licking my bald head like a lollipop. Not sure how hygienic that would be considered, but my body was already filled to the brim with toxic matter, so what additional harm could it muster? I woke up one morning to find a CSI crime scene of blood up and down the walls in the bedroom. Coco had chewed her tail with anxiety to such an extent that I needed to take her to the vet. It had to be shaved. The vet said he had 'never seen anything like that before,' a headline to my life so far. I was given a course of antibiotics for her to follow. There would now be two of us in recovery.

The following day, our patient numbers swelled, and we would officially be the special needs family. I woke up to find Daisy the puppy had vomited wombat poo everywhere; Miss Lipstick had croup and needed to go to the doctors, and shortly after, Mr Mac would become ill too. I had to perfect my mothering skills at arm's length with a face mask. They tell you to avoid being around sick people, a little difficult when they live with you, and you are solo parenting.

Eventually, everyone returned to school. I even managed a cheeky weekend alone (at home of course) before chemo round three. This helped me to recover, or at least be back upright. I was beginning to be monitored more closely and was moved from the open plan treatment bays to a separate side room with its own bed. My anxiety was reaching new heights and being noticed by others. I had been sent a warm blanket over by a friend and would take it with me so I could make the room feel a bit more homely.

The therapy dogs were doing the rounds that day. It was suggested that a particular one pay me a visit. I laughed when even the dog refused to set foot in the room. The majority of flooring at the centre was carpet. My side room had vinyl flooring and its texture was a step too far for him. I'm not sure who was more determined that he still visited. The volunteer laid down a towel and placed him on it. He was slid across towards me for a pat. His visit made my day. That night, a friend took the children out for pizza. It was a reprieve for us all. I loved that they could continue to have glimpses of the outside world when I could not. I, on the other hand, slept for 20 hours and ate anti-nausea tablets like smarties.

I volunteered to be in a commercial for a cancer fundraising campaign. The director was a friend and our Bondi friends' group would be filmed together as one of the stories. I had previously worked for a large cancer organisation, so I knew how hard it was to get patients during treatment to be part of campaigns. I was also so grateful to the charity for the services they had recently provided. I was happy to play my part—Cancer, Models own. It would be a chance also to thank the Bondi mums who supplied food to us. It was two weeks before my fourth and final round of chemo. I had not travelled further than from my house to the cancer centre around the corner, so I totally underestimated how exhausting the journey alone would be. Two friends from a previous job came down to visit me earlier that day for lunch. One of them offered to drive us up to the city. The children would be with their dad that weekend and I would be filming that night. It was my first weekend away from home.

I'd predominately been wearing trackie pants the last few months, so I wasn't sure what they wanted this cancer patient to look like. Fashionable or casual? Sick, but still hopeful? The filming was taking place at someone's house. One of the bedrooms was the dressing room. A make-up lady was on standby, so at least I could be made to look a bit livelier. I must have looked tired as without thinking, she started to put whitening drops in my eyes. I yelped in pain. My eyeballs were arid, so it felt like she'd used paint stripper.

I rumbled through my overnight bag looking for outfit options. Of course, I'd packed a mix of last-minute items chosen with the following in mind—clean or at the very least, semi-clean and secondly, did they fit or could they be stretched to fit. Future note to self: do not choose to wear a bat-winged top for your cancer debut on national television. If the screen makes you look 10Ibs heavier anyway, that top will require a wide-angle lens. I had the option to wear nothing on my head, but I was already feeling vulnerable. My friend gave me a silk scarf to wear and the decision was made. I did, however, forget to take off my bright orange Fitbit wristband. I only wore it to track my sleep and not my step count. I wondered if anyone else saw it and thought it bizarre.

It would be the first time that this group of friends had seen me. They may have seen the odd post on Facebook, but it's more confronting in the flesh. If I had barely got used to seeing me so swollen and bald, how could they be expected to? One of my friends had lost her mother to breast cancer and I knew she was finding it hard to be around me. I made a special effort to seek her out so that we could talk away from everyone. We took refuge in the most intimate of sanctums for women—the bathroom. Behind the closed doors, I showed her my scar as if I was showing a holiday snap. It was the first time I had shown anyone. I'm not sure if I thought that showing her my scar would somehow help her heal or me start to process.

As the night progressed, I was finding it harder to breathe. I was constantly fanning myself as if I was on fire. I felt self-conscious being featured, especially after seeing the sadness in my friends' eyes. I could tell that some were struggling. On the other hand, some with good intentions would overcompensate with left-field reactions.

'I *know exactly* what you are going through ... I've had a breast reduction,' offered a lady I just met that night.

'*Everyone* I know has had cancer ... *I'll* probably have cancer,' offered another in a show of solidarity. Her delivery was more exuberant than Oprah—'You get cancer, you get cancer, we all get cancer.'

'Oh, breast cancer ... Yes, that's a good cancer to get,' offered another.

No. Not really. **Not** having cancer would be better.

We all say ill-considered things when we are nervous or don't know what to say. I get it, I've said more than a reasonable amount of classic lines over the years that I cringe about now. At the end of the day, we are all human. The important thing is to admit when you are having difficulty knowing what to say.

I hadn't been around such a hive of activity and noise for months. I took a few short breaks and drank lots of water, to get me through the long hours of filming. I smiled as selfies were taken in between scenes. Everyone was checking the shots to see how their hair looked. Upside? Well, I had none to check, just needed to keep dabbing those beads of sweat. I couldn't slip away quietly like at a party. I'd over-committed myself as I always did. The shoot didn't end till later that night and I was taken back to my hotel room by a close friend. She ironed my outfit for the next day as we chatted and digested the evening's events. My limbs felt like lead and I barely stirred. After she left the sound of silence was deafening. I fell asleep almost instantly.

I arose like a sloth from my bed the next morning. My room was overlooking the beach and I was transfixed by the view. This had been my old stomping ground. Now, I was just passing through. I took a shower and was confronted by my aged reflection. I wanted to call back the make-up artist. I would need to use double strength under-eye cover-up to look alive. I was due to meet a friend and my old neighbour for brunch. It was so lovely to see them, but I felt quite reckless and exposed in the busy cafe. I had been playing it so safe back home and not mixed with many people for such a long time, it was jarring to be in such a contrasting environment.

A car had been ordered to drive me back home. A brief hello to the driver and I completely crashed out on the back seat. I don't remember any of the journey or how long it took. I went straight to bed when I got home. My temperature started to rise.

It's hard to know if you are going to act too soon (it's just a flush) or too late (it's spiked, call an ambulance). I held out until later the next day. My temperature was going in one direction only—up. The children were in the car heading back with their dad when I called. I was on speakerphone, so I tried to sound lighthearted.

'I'm just going to pop into the hospital to get some antibiotics.'

It was a Sunday so the emergency department would be the only place open. It provided a good cover story to prevent any alarm bells from being raised in the children's minds. To be honest, I hadn't really thought it was that serious. I just rocked up to the ER in what I was wearing. After confirming my details and that I was between chemotherapies I was taken straight into triage. I'd never had that happen before. After my initial stats were taken, an intravenous cannula was immediately put in. A bag of antibiotics was administered and supplemental oxygen through a nasal cannula. I'm not sure what my stats were to prompt such swift action, but it was easier not to ask questions. I was then informed that I would need to be admitted to a ward and wouldn't be leaving for at least three days. *Whaat? Three* days?? What would I do with the children, they were on their way? Who would take care of the dogs?

I didn't have any spare clothes, so I called a friend to collect some things. Luckily, I had given spare keys out to friends like they were going out of fashion. I was more worried that the children would be passed on to her if she was there when they were dropped off. I suggested she grab my weekend bag as I hadn't had the energy to unpack it yet. It had all my toiletries still in it, so was ready to go. I forgot that it was filled with choices for a TV shoot—silver shoes and evening wear—not really practical for a hospital stay. I knew their father wouldn't readily volunteer to have the children return with him, so I just asked him to stay overnight at our house. I would have to figure out the next bit later on. For now, I just needed to breathe. Let's make me even more puffed up please—bring on the steroids. I was wheeled up into a single room and an oxygen mask and an ECG heart monitor connected. The concern was that I might have a blood clot on my lungs. I'd have to wait till the next morning to have an ultrasound for confirmation. It wouldn't be a restful night.

I became the girl in a bubble. No-one was allowed in or out without a mask and disposable gowns. It was frightening and an ominous precursor to COVID-19 days to come. My stomach was beginning to look like a deflating balloon as pungent toxins were released. The door was left open, but I'm not sure if that was to save my blushes or for additional air circulation.

I was lent some hospital scrubs to wear as PJs. As I arrived for the CT scan the next day, the technician asked if I had just come off my hospital shift. Mate, I can barely breathe, much less look after patients. The children missed school and were bought to see me. I sounded more like Darth Vader than their mum. I had to negotiate with their father to take them for a few days. I had to keep looking at the bigger picture. I called their school to let them know of the changes and arranged for someone to help with the dogs. I berated myself for exposing myself to the elements and endangering my treatment plan. I was frightened and alone. I didn't want to die in a hospital surrounded by strangers.

Numerous bags of antibiotics and saline were drip-fed over the next few days. My temperature slowly came down. Another burst of steroids allowed me to finally breathe properly. It was not an easy time, being confined to that room with just my thoughts. On the third day before I was due to leave the hospital, Mr Mac called pleading to come home. I was his safe haven and rock. Unfortunately, Miss Lipstick had a cough. I couldn't risk getting sick again. I needed more time to recover from this bout. It was hard for them to understand, but like a boxing bag, I needed to be upright so I could be knocked back down.

July 1, 2015 was my final round of chemo. This time, I went alone. Back to the same side room and in a fitting full-circle moment, I was visited by Angus, the same therapy dog from my first time. My three months of chemo treatment had finally ended.

I left clutching my certificate of completion from the hospital. It was the most life-affirming one I would ever receive.

It was also laminated.

16

Radioactive, Radioactive

The aftershocks from my last round of chemo were brutal. I felt tired and tested. I was aching and throbbing, and my bone pain would creep up when I least expected. I needed to be gentle with myself, but I also needed to get through two weeks of school holidays. There would be no reprieve this time as their father would be away in Germany. The day I said goodbye to the nurses at the cancer centre, I remarked how amazing it was that I had avoided losing my eyebrows. Nurse Nurture smiled knowingly and told me to just wait and see. I remained hopeful of making it into that medical journal.

My excitement turned to horror about a week or so later when I caught a glimpse of myself in the car mirror. I looked like something from Star Trek. I needed to revert to my Look Good, Feel Better bag of tricks, for a solution. If only I could remember how they showed us. I casually entered the children's playroom to see if they would notice my eyebrow handiwork.

Quick as a flash, Mr Mac looked up and said,

'Mummy you look like a man, trying to look like a woman.'

I burst out laughing. I guess I needed more practice then. I still struggle today to make them look even, so when you see me, please be kind.

Before my chemo ended, I had to meet with the next member of my treatment team, the radiation oncologist. I was now working towards part two of my treatment—radiotherapy. Essentially, it beams high doses of radiation to kill cancer cells and shrink tumours. I knew low doses of radiation are used in X-rays, but I wasn't familiar with how this type worked. There is a whole other set of statistics that informs the duration of your course, the dosage and the width of the treatment area. The purpose of my radiotherapy treatment was to eliminate any left behind cancer cells. I imagined that if radiotherapy was a person, he would be the Publican shouting, 'Last drinks please'. He would lock the doors and walk around the premises, waking up the last stragglers at the bar. Then, he would mop the floor of any last-minute cancer spillages. After I had met my radiotherapy oncologist, I received a copy of the letter he wrote to my oncologist with an update. I couldn't help but marvel at his description of me:

'Thanks for asking me to see this 44-year-old **pre-menopausal single mother** *with two children, aged 11 and 9, the oldest having Asperger's disease…* **Alopecia** *consistent with chemotherapy…* **moderate to large-sized breasts**…*'*

Well, if that isn't an opener for an online dating profile, I don't know what is! On the bright side, my breasts were noted as being rather remarkable.

Radioactive, Radioactive

I had just a few weeks to recalibrate and adjust to my new zombie features and the fact that I would need to travel further afield for my next batch of treatments. The machinery for my *Star Wars* treatment was at another cancer centre about a 40-minute drive from home. I would need sixteen sessions over six weeks. It would play havoc on my social life. Oh, that's right I didn't have one.

I was offered access to free community transport. There was a bus that drove from the local hospital to the cancer centre where the radiotherapy machines were. I couldn't shake the dark imagery of us all lining up to go on the bus, a roll call being taken, and a few members would no longer be with us. The rest of us would set off, full of beans and singing, as if on a Contiki Tour ride. On the return home journey, we would all be slunk in our seats in silence as the after-effects would set in. Being faced with your own potential death was one thing but as a group activity? I didn't think I could face that. I was more of a solo flyer in my pain. In the end, the decision was out of my hands as it required a block booking of appointments. This meant everyone had to wait until the last person had finished their treatment. I couldn't be guaranteed to be back in time for the end of school, so it was a nonstarter.

I drove myself up to have my induction and to get some tattoos. Tattoos, not in a badass mother kind of way, but small black dots to ensure the machine accurately lined up the area for the beams to be directed towards. They are permanent reminders long after treatment ends. Of course, one of mine would be positioned at the centre of my cleavage. It is often mistaken for a pen mark, mole, or fleck of dust.

I was led into a side room by the radiology nurse for my induction. Whilst they were looking at my notes, I sat uneasily in the chair.

Another ground zero stage and confronting mix of not knowing what to expect, new staff, new machinery, new lingo and a new location. I sat quietly waiting for us to start. The inaction and lack of movement galvanised my mind into freefall. As I reflected on how far I had come, the reality of how much more was still to come engulfed me. Silent tears cascaded. My breathing quickened and my shoulders started shaking. The nurse scooted her chair towards me and held my hand.

Travel and treatment became too much for me to do alone. I reached out on Facebook to ask for help with the drive. I was worried that I might have already exhausted everyone's kindness. I was humbled by people's generous offers. Why was it still so hard to ask?

Cancer is a tricky one. Most people know *someone* who has experienced a type of cancer. Like pregnancy, everybody has an opinion. I remember when my son was born, I was so overcome with the intensity of becoming a new mother that I didn't trust my own instinct. When I was first pregnant, I was habitually told that I was either too large or too small and even asked if I was having twins. It was open season. It was worse when my baby was born. Strangers informed me that he looked too cold or how he might be crying because he was hungry. I learnt the best response was to say, 'What works for Mr Mac is …' You couldn't really argue with that. Sometimes, it feels that way with cancer or treatment. It can become a competitive or comparison laden subject.

'Oh, radiotherapy will be a *breeze* compared to chemo…'

'My <insert friend, spouse, sibling, relative, someone they saw on TV> *drove themselves* to *all* their appointments. *Then*, they went to (insert work, childcare, up a mountain, gave birth) afterwards.'

Radioactive, Radioactive

If you state your treatment is different or try to explain your circumstances, it might appear you are defensive. My advice? Nod politely and say that it was helpful. Everyone's circumstances are different, but also, none of us really know how our body is going to react to the twist and turns of the treatment path. Let alone how we will emotionally endure the entire length of treatment.

In the beginning, the drive to the sessions, the waiting, the set-up, positioning and repositioning on the machinery for the 15–20 minutes of radiotherapy laser beam treatment, didn't seem too bad. It was the accumulation of all these things day-in and day-out that I found the most gruelling. Ironic that from the outside, even though I was still bald, I looked better than I did during chemo. Below the surface, under the light cover of a shirt, I would be raw, steadily burning and developing blisters.

Day two and I was already depleted. My ambition to complete the first week of travel by myself may not have been the brightest idea. I was, however, regaining some daily structure with the children. Family dinner became a regular occurrence at the table again. Damn, there was no-one around to see that major step forward.

The children were beginning to be more open with me again. I'd resumed the nightly routine of sitting on their beds chatting with them individually: a chance for them to share their days and any worries. Miss Lipstick was struggling to get comfortable in her bed one night. I was about to leave her room when something she said stopped me in my tracks.

'I wish you had pranked me about breast cancer.'

I slowly turned around. I tried to look unruffled as I sat back down. I knew there would be more revelations to come if Miss Lipstick was given a chance.

'You've given me the spell of breast cancer,' she added.

My heart shattered. She wasn't entirely wrong. I had been advised that she would need breast cancer checks from the age of 30. She was not aware of this, but it had weighed heavily on me since I had been told. In survival mode, there is short supply of time to be fully present and available to everyone. I had covered the basics of a functioning mum but had limited bandwidth to hold space for the children to process what was happening. I didn't even know how to do this for myself. At that moment, I felt I had let her down.

I hesitated as I wasn't sure which question I should answer first. I started with the last.

'You know that *my* mummy didn't have breast cancer? So, it doesn't mean you will either,' I gently assured her.

'It must have been such a hard time for you,' I added, holding her hands. 'You've been so *very* brave.'

Her eyes filled with tears. The swirl of her trapped emotions was palpable. We'd barely touched the tip. That night I gave her a journal to capture her questions in, so we could go through them together. I didn't want her to think that just because I was tired, I was not interested. I also thought it might be a less confronting way for her to release some of the turmoil inside. It was a temporary solution, but I needed to at least give her some peace to sleep that night. I enrolled her into a local children's anxiety group program so that she would have another outlet outside of the family. I wasn't sure how much she would share, but she would be taught some tools to help. I continued to suck in my own emotions. The time to dwell or process would have to come later.

At the end of the first week of radiotherapy, some friends from overseas returned. They were staying in the area with their two daughters—the youngest was my goddaughter. They invited us over for dinner. It was our first family social outing in months. I had started a hormonal (endocrine) treatment, Zoladex, to switch off my ovaries from making oestrogen. This monthly injection prompted a second version of menopause. Same same, but different. There was no gradual and demure introduction to menopause symptoms with this switch on and off method. Instead, you are thrown headfirst into extreme and unpredictable flushing, weight gain, and the joyous 'menopausal slumber' of two hours asleep, 10 minutes awake and repeat till morning. Hot and bothered don't cover it. You effectively become a walking volcano with the clarity of an insomniac. I could only counter this by wearing light layers of clothing like choux pastry, ready to be peeled off when required.

I started burning up as soon as I arrived. I was worried if I took my beanie off, the girls would be shocked. I held on until I could bear it no longer. I needed to rip it off. I managed to pre-warn them that it might look a bit scary before my final reveal. They both looked at me for a moment and then went off to continue to play their games with my kids. That's the beauty of children, tell them what it is, let them see what it is, then they just move on.

I've always been the frivolous all singing and dancing fun aunty/godmother, so I got up to shake my thang with the children that night. I promptly had to sit back down. If this is week one into radiotherapy, then Houston, we might have a problem.

I cried at the beginning of the second week when I found more sprouts of hair populating my head. They had progressed from the downy hair of a newborn to a fuller coverage. This precious cargo didn't go unnoticed by other family members. Miss Lipstick even wrote a poem for me:

> **'My mum has a twinkle in her eyes. When the sun hits her eyes, I haven't seen a single time when she doesn't have that beautiful big long smile on her face.**
>
> **Her tears are like lemon drops and hardly come out of their socik <socket>**
>
> **her little baby hair and head shine in the dark and her eyes are as blue as the sky (on a sunny day at lest <least>) I love her if she was a <an> animal she would be a beautiful dove with sparkly wings.'**

It appeared that radiotherapy was a less scary concept for the children and the house was once again full of laughter and children singing at the top of their lungs:

Whoa, whoa, I'm radioactive, radioactive,
Whoa, whoa, I'm radioactive, radioactive.

Good times.

Radioactive, Radioactive

School open days, puppy accidents, and general daily life shenanigans filled the intervals between radiotherapy sessions. I tried to ride this wave of normality by creating a Wish Jar filled with ideas from the children of things we could do on the weekends. The first wish selected was for a family trip to the cinema to see *Ant-Man*. Mr Mac secretly invited three other friends to join us. Fair play to him. You have to grab on to normal when you can.

The weekdays continued to be filled with treatments and other follow-up appointments. This cancer business was a full-time job. There was also a continuous exchange of paperwork and endless filling in of forms. I wondered how others had managed to work full time and continue treatment. At an appointment with Dr Familiar, we had to complete a form (I don't remember what for), but I will never forget the question:

Is the illness for a 24-month period? Terminal or unknown?

Dr Familiar ticked 'unknown'.

Gulp.

I became the kid in the backseat of the car yelling, 'Are we nearly there yet?' The monotony of the therapy was beginning to wear me right down.

I was relieved to receive a call one morning to cancel the radiotherapy session. The machine had broken down. I had woken up with such severe pain and a splitting headache that I'd arranged an emergency appointment with my chiropractor. I needed to relieve the discomfort enough that I could tolerate driving myself to treatment and back. The call had come in just before I was about to turn on to the highway.

I returned home, pulled back the curtains and slept. This became the new routine after each session. In the door, pop some pills, haul myself back to bed and sleep for a couple of hours. If my appointment was scheduled late, I'd leave the front door unlocked so the children could slip in quietly and grab themselves a snack until I woke up.

I had a love-hate relationship with that radiation therapy machine. I hadn't realised that the pillow I was lying on during the initial measurements, became a mould to ensure I always lay on the bed in the same position. I was so nervous that day, I must have been lying with a twisted spine. Now for each treatment, I would have to repeat that same awkward pose with arms held above my head. It was a game of horizontal musical statues as the machine moved into position and precision laser beams streamed out. I would close my eyes to disengage. Not enough time to drift to sleep, but sufficient to unplug my mind. A couple of days later, the machine broke again—twice—whilst I was lying underneath it. It was incredibly uncomfortable as I had to grip the bars above my head whilst the technician worked his magic to reset it. Similar to dangling off monkey bars carrying my entire body weight. No easy feat.

One weekend, at the halfway point, some girlfriends from Bondi visited. They arrived with some more cooked meals and treats. I was so excited to see them both and show them the local markets, held at the children's school. Just after the entranceway to the market, they stopped to lean over and look at some engraved bricks on the school grounds. I thought I must have pointed them out as Mr Mac, and Miss Lipstick's engraved bricks were there too. I continued to walk on after Miss Lipstick, but when I turned around, I noticed they were still there deep in conversation.

'Isn't it terrible?'

'What?' I interrupted.

'Three children from the same family.'

'What?' I repeated.

'And just six years old.'

I finally twigged. My friends were looking at the dates of each brick as if it referred to the number of years the child had *lived* and not the years they *attended* the school. I'm not sure where the miscommunication came from. After explaining it was a school fundraiser and *not* a cemetery, we were all crying with laughter.

As we were leaving the markets to return home, we decided to get some drinks for lunch from the local bottle shop drive-through.

'Beers or wine?' one of the girls asked.

'Mummy you've got beers in the garage,' Miss Lipstick piped up from the back seat.

'*No, I don't*' I replied indignantly.

'*Yes, you do*,' she implored. Then, she continued with the fateful words. 'For the men that don't come.'

This prompted us all to burst into raucous laughter once more. I had long forgotten that I had some beers in the back fridge. I'd bought them to give to a friend's partner for helping in the garden. Clearly, Miss Lipstick had not. Although she may have been confused by why we had laughed about her factual observation of the beers, it created such a sheer moment of joy that kept me smiling throughout the weeks ahead. There is no greater tonic than laughter. It sets you up to face anything.

Miss Lipstick continued to keep my spirits up when she gave me another beautiful card with the following words:

'Hi, mum,

I love you very very much and sometimes I think you don't know that and also if you wanted to know you are the best mum ever, I could not want more than you. You are full of intersting \<interesting\> things. I know that I don't talk about you \<your\> illness much it's because it a horrable \<horrible\> thing to talk about. I also don't like to see \<you\> in pain of struggling Please don't forget I love you very much xxx love Miss Lipstick - Get well soon.

Fun fact, radiotherapy has an accumulative effect. The burning continues two weeks *after* your last treatment. In the final weeks, my breast looked like it was suffering from pubescent acne. The rash from radiation was unbearably itchy and hot. It now had to be wrapped with petroleum gauze after each treatment. I smelled like an oil rig. I also had perfected the side hug to avoid pressing on the wound—nothing like a lovely shade of first-degree burns to keep you sleeping on your back. I'm an avid side sleeper so I could only dream of returning to those days. Sometimes it's the little things you miss.

August 19, 2015 was my last day of radiotherapy.

17

The Aftermath

After six months of prodding and poking, I enjoyed a ceasefire from the gruelling treatment. I lifted my head above the parapet to survey the damage. Aftershocks were engraved in my body and soul. I had a swollen frame, scars, burns, and felt stripped to my core. Even my precious little stubbly shoots were painful as they grew. They made my head feel like it had been doused with ice water. Every time the wind caught them, they stung like open wounds. My body was decimated on the outside, but the real damage was on the inside. I just wasn't ready to address that yet. The longer-lasting effects are buried deep in the terms and conditions.

There was another way I could proactively stack the survival odds in my favour. It would require the removal of my ovaries to prevent the production of oestrogen. If I revisited the hysterectomy option, I could also remove a potential side effect of taking Tamoxifen—uterine cancer. The operation from earlier in the year would now boomerang back onto the agenda, albeit a more extreme version—a radical hysterectomy via C-section. I was still all about efficiencies, so I'd asked to tag on that pesky umbilical hernia for good measure.

In the blink of an eye, the purpose of the original surgery had gone from pain-saving to lifesaving.

I weighed up the best timing for the operation. I could have waited longer but decided to rip the band-aid off. A bit like determining the right age gap between siblings. If my year had virtually been wiped out already, why not make it my very own 'Annus Horribilis'. I could then start the new year afresh. The family relay of support continued. My mother, who I affectionately refer to as 'the Duchess', was booked to come over to help me manage the aftermath. It would be the first time she had ever visited us in Australia. She has high standards and expectations, so I was a little nervous about living up to them.

I believe that no matter what stage or type of cancer you have, the fear whilst waiting for the diagnosis is similar for everyone. The destruction from the treatment, process to rebuild and your mental outlook (especially after treatment ends) is individualised. No-one, except the person going through it, can ever really know what it's like for them. Like grief, only time will tell how long a person needs to process and heal. All you can do is provide them with a safe haven, space, support and compassion. A great starting point is to simply ask the person what help they might need. Or better still, unsolicited offers like dropping off food, or posting unexpected care packages can really brighten up the day. Just don't get offended if they want to be alone or don't respond to your texts instantly. Even offering your company and sitting with them can be a boost. For me it was the little gestures and thoughts that meant so much. The aftermath period is just as important as the treatment treadmill time. It can feel a bit like the days and weeks after a funeral when the guests have left the building and only you remain. Still standing, but on shaky legs with no idea how to move forward. This can be the most critical time to check-in.

The Aftermath

My priority for the next few months was to rebuild my physical wellbeing before the final operation. I knew I was starting from a low baseline and took a dual approach: exercise and nutrition. I hadn't considered my mental health at this stage. Earlier in the year, I had started to reduce my antidepressants to half a dose. The weaning process came to an abrupt halt when I was diagnosed. I was advised to put any ideas for further reduction on the backburner. I would neither revisit this option now nor spend time processing what I'd just been through. It remained in the 'too-hard basket'.

I joined a local gym. I was measured, weighed, and provided a tailored program to follow. There's nothing like standing in Lycra in front of strangers to get you motivated. I was hastily trying to kickstart my recovery. Had I learnt nothing from my CrossFit attempt? I was teetering between wanting to fall under the radar and speeding ahead to be part of the masses. 'Be patient. Be gentle with yourself,' I would beseech. I would compassionately offer this advice to anyone else, but it was harder to accept from myself. The truth was, I was just so tired of *looking sick* and feeling sick of looking *so tired*.

I didn't need to utter the words 'mirror, mirror on the wall' to know the answer.

I would only know if my treatments were successful at the first mammogram in seven months. It was a long time for the jury to be out. I was struggling to see someone I recognised. I felt frumpy and unfeminine and desperate to look like myself again. I was only at the start of a myriad of hairstyles before then. I was frustrated that my hair wasn't growing at the pace of Play-doh hair heads. At that time, I was sporting a perfect middle runway strip on my crown with small tufts of hair on either side. It was like the reverse

Brazilian. I'd never wanted the option of a comb-over so much. My hair colour was a mix of black and white, like a badger. To complete the look, I had a combination of crop circles and moss coverage with an overtone of fluff at the back. How many cowlicks can one girl have on her head? It appeared in my case, never too many. Also, no-one tells you that when your hair does start to grow, it will begin at a point halfway up your head. Lucky for me, that was slightly above a huge red birthmark, I never knew I had. It would be a while longer before I could put hair clips in.

It was now springtime. My heavier beanie look was not going to cut it anymore. I found a stylish lighter knit type of beanie at the local markets. I was thrilled with my new purchase. It was just the pop of summer colour I needed. The first time I wore it was at the dog park. An older gentleman approached me and asked if I had Leukaemia. #Fashionfail. As if my disappointment had been felt in the universe, the following day a surprise package was left hanging at my front door. A 'Très Jolie' and stylish hat was inside. It resembled something that the elusive Parisian chemo patient might wear. I called the shop listed on the tag to find out who I should thank. I was deeply moved to find out it was from the property manager of our rental. Her daughters were at the same school. It put a huge smile on my face each time I put it on and was a wonderful reminder that we were still in people's thoughts.

Going through treatment, I was advised it would be counterproductive to introduce antioxidant foods into my diet as they might interfere with the chemotherapy. I could now move forward and was invited to attend a workshop at the Cancer Centre to find out more about nutrition and self-care. It was the first time I had really contemplated the word self-care in any positive light. It had always felt too much like self-ish to make yourself a priority. I was under this

The Aftermath

false illusion that as a single mother with a child on the autism spectrum, my life was precoded for struggle. The reality could not be farther from the truth. I needed to make self-care (or I prefer self-nurture) a priority. It would not only mean I had more energy and love to give, it would also make me a better mum and carer. Rome wasn't built in a day, and neither would I be. These new tools would be trial and error. Introducing changes starts with unlearning old patterns, overcoming resistance and consistency to enmesh new ones.

A charity that provided holiday accommodation to families going through cancer offered us a holiday home to use. We were thrilled at the prospect of a few days away. We had been cocooned in our house for too long. With much excitement, we started packing ahead of time—a new concept for me. That is, Miss Lipstick and I did, Mr Mac just ran around the house sporting a plaster as a moustache. He'd cut his own hair at school the day prior, so he looked like he had a friar tuck haircut. Allegedly, he'd been bored. Good to know that there would be two members of the household sporting crewcuts.

We stayed in a house in a small hamlet on the South Coast of New South Wales. It was just a few hours' drive away, near the beach and with no Wi-fi or mobile reception. A chance for the family to just hang out, play endless hours of Dr Who Monopoly, walk on the beach and enjoy fresh air and a change of scenery. It was the furthest I'd been away from the house and the perfect cure to cabin fever. I received a surprise package just before we left with shorts and matching swimming rashie (top). I had briefly mentioned to a friend that I was self-conscious about being in a swimsuit again. I also needed to keep my chest covered to prevent further burning. I was so touched by her thoughtfulness. I savoured being able to dip my toes in the sea and just be. Although out of season, we had plenty to entertain us. I even managed to jump on the trampoline at the playground. I nearly passed out. It was signs of life that the children needed to see and that I did too. It was also the first time I'd felt carefree again and could glimpse a light at the end of the tunnel. It was the break we all needed.

I unexpectedly received a call to join a free breast cancer exercise program to help restore mobility and relieve treatment side effects. At first, I tried to decline as I felt I'd already received more than my fair share of support from the community. By all accounts, this had been the automatic response from all attendees. It appears those that needed a boost to their self-esteem the most, were the most challenging group to recruit. After a bit of further encouragement, I accepted a place. I was so glad that I did. I hadn't realised how much the scarring under my arm and radiotherapy had restricted my movement. The program provided information sessions and steps to reintroduce gentle exercises both in and out of the swimming pool. The program coincided with a need to shave my legs again. I hadn't been this excited since I was a teenager.

The group provided a nurturing and safe space for people who had been through this journey. It was a chance to learn even more about nutrition, self-care and wellbeing. It provided strategies for recovery and a new way of living. It was the first time that I admitted that fear was holding me back and that I was struggling with who I was now.

I was the only one with no hair in the group. It was the first time I dared to take my hat off in public. Well, I probably would have looked a bit ridiculous wearing a beanie in the pool. I was curious to see all the different textures and stages of hair regrowth amongst the

The Aftermath

group—obsessed much Louise? I'd heard of people's hair growing back differently to how their hair was before chemo. Fondly referred to as 'chemo curls' I wondered what that might look like. I leant over to one of the attendees.

'Hi, sorry to ask something so personal, is your hair texture from chemo?' I asked awkwardly

'No,' she replied, 'This is my natural hair.'

'Oh yes sorry, it's lovely,' I replied, removing my foot from my mouth.

The program continued for several more weeks. It showed me the importance of surrounding yourself with like-minded people. It was a chance to talk, learn practical skills and kept me buoyant during those weeks. I started to prioritise self-care and learnt how to do daily stretching, mindfulness, gentle exercise options, and much more. I'd been missing the structure of treatment, but this was *more* than that. It emphasised the importance of *maintaining your wellbeing*. I saw looking after myself as something *temporary*. A *passive* requirement *only* activated when you were not well. I saw my recovery as the final destination point. However, wellbeing requires a *proactive* approach, not only to avoid being sick in the future but to be able to create a more vital life. Seeds for future changes were planted.

I was asked to speak about the program on the local radio station to encourage other people to reach out. I happily accepted.

It was the first time I had been able to stretch my professional marketing muscles again and relished the opportunity. I met with the team leader before our slot to provide her with some encouragement. I hadn't even considered prepping myself on what I should say before we were due on air. I was used to speaking professionally about other people and products. I'd only be asked questions about my own experience. How hard could it be?

The radio host graciously introduced us, and the team leader answered her questions. I was busy ticking off the checklist of points we'd discussed beforehand. I wasn't prepared when the conversation quickly changed direction. It started off well. I was asked what had brought me to the program. Cancer. Tick. But as soon as I was asked to tell my own story, sheer terror consumed me.

'The program was really good at helping me stretch out the *scars* from the lymph node removal under my arm … my *scars*,' I repeated, 'my *scars* were really cut deep.' … God help me, I couldn't stop saying the bloody word. I was caught in an endless loop on live radio. I was mortified.

I'd built a career on using words, written or spoken. How could I stumble so much? Was I still suffering from chemo brain? I was at a loss to find *my own words* for *my own experience*. I may have resilience in spades, but emotionally I was only lightly stitched together. I could not face seeing my scars in the mirror. I couldn't speak coherently about them or see them as part of myself and not extensions of someone else. I could not see them as battles won nor contemplate their roots deeply etched within.

18

There's No Womb at the Inn

The countdown to the end of the year had begun. The last school term would be especially memorable as it would be Mr Mac's final year at primary school. The possibility of seeing him start high school was now within reach. Our trip away had anchored our family bond.

I was now well over the halfway mark of treatment. The hormone therapy regime was back under the wise counsel of Dr Calm. There were a couple of ways to proceed. Either start Tamoxifen medication (usually for pre-menopausal women), or trial an aromatase inhibitor—Arimidex, Aromasin or Femara (for postmenopausal women). I was placed in the latter group and started to take an aromatase inhibitor tablet each day. This was in addition to the hormonal (endocrine) treatment monthly injection which I still had to take until my operation. Effectively, I was now taking dual medication.

Although a natural process of getting older is a reduction in hormones, this blitz approach caused a rapid increase in menopause symptoms. I weathered fatigue, sleep disturbances, brain fog, memory loss and severe joint pain and bone aches. I could hardly get up in the morning to help the children before school. I was frustrated at this pseudo mother state. On the outside, things were slightly more agreeable. My eyes had returned some of their sparkle.

We trialled another version of an aromatase inhibitor to see if my symptoms were more a tail end effect of radiotherapy. I enquired about the medication's possible side effects. My oncologist made me laugh when he quietly mentioned that one of them, though unlikely, was facial hair. Being a bearded AND bald lady was not that appealing, but I persevered.

Traditional methods to alleviate harsh symptoms of menopause were to use additional hormones. This could prove risky for me as my breast cancer cells were hormone-sensitive and we were trying to neutralise traces. I may have won a trophy for completing my cancer treatments, but the tradeoff was living with atrophy. I would have to look at other solutions for that later down the line. Any additional chance to live would surely be worth it.

I tried to increase my movement with weights at the gym, swimming, walks, and pottering in the garden. I'd changed my diet. My pantry was a nod to hemp seeds and powdered supplements. I tried to shift some of the extra weight caused by the steroids and menopause to see if it would ease the joints. Nothing appeared to work or maybe I didn't give it enough time. A multitude of adverse reactions and the double-barrelled medical menopause proved to be too tough an assignment to tackle. My body needed time to adjust. We needed to see if things would settle down on their own. I continued on the monthly injection but had a break from the daily tablets. We agreed to meet in early December, the day before my operation, to draw up a new plan of attack.

My recovery was an uneasy dance. A few steps forward and a few steps back. It's hard to comprehend the relief and responsibility that having a second chance at living gives a person. Let alone someone who already wasn't sure what changes were needed or how to make them. I wanted to do life better. I didn't want to waste my chance to regroup, re-evaluate, and reboot. Surely there had to be a reason why I was the one still standing? There would be no time to unpack these feelings now. I just needed to buckle down and simply concentrate on surviving this next operation. Limping to the end of the year would be my next milestone. I wasn't sure then, but I was beginning to show signs of survivor's guilt.

In the lead up to my mother's arrival, I was back to updating my checklists and contact details. I had not seen my mother since my last trip to England over a year prior. The visits from my sisters seemed like a lifetime ago. Unbeknownst to me, my mother's own health had begun to decline before her visit. She had recently packed up two houses, relocated from France back to England and endured a stay in hospital in between. She would break up the journey in South Africa, staying with my sister Ann. Despite of all these setbacks, she had been determined to come. I doubt either of us could have foreseen how tiring the trip alone would be for her. I was just grateful she came and excited for her to see where we lived and the home I had made for our family.

She was always the inspiration for keeping a beautiful and inviting home. The timing of her visit also meant that she would be able to attend some of the children's end of year school events including Mr Mac leaving primary school. My mother had only been with my children a handful of times over the years. Having her be here to see Mr Mac's key milestone was even more special.

My cousin picked my mother up from the airport. She stayed with her in Sydney that first night. They arrived the next day ahead of my oncology appointment. It was an opportunity to meet the team and show them the hospital where I'd spent so many hours.

The meeting started with a flurry of introductions. Discussions moved on to my medication regime. As soon as the oncologist started to present alternate options, my mother interrupted and turned to me and said,

'I think you're being very negative.'

I could feel my nerves prickling. My heart sunk. Could she not see how hard I had battled to get to this point? I felt unfairly judged. I took a sharp intake of breath, turned to face her, and tried to explain.

'Mum, I *literally* couldn't open up my hands and fingers or get out of bed to help the children in the morning,' I spikily replied.

The need to justify simmered, but I didn't want to make a scene. Our family was good at that. The oncologist continued and we agreed that I would try Tamoxifen in January. I was relieved to have an extended break where I would no longer need to have those bone-freezing monthly injections. I felt my life force was already being slowly sucked away like marrow from a bone. I worried I'd end up looking like a raisin, a fat one, so maybe more like a prune.

As we made our way back to the car, my cousin could see, I was still reeling from my mother's comment.

'She kept saying how she couldn't wait to see you at dinner last night,' she offered as consolation.

My eager show and tell efforts had fallen flat. I felt like a child again yearning to be heard and seeking approval. I felt I would never quite meet expectations.

We returned home, and my cousin left.

That night was presentation night at school. I'm not sure what time it would have been for my mother's body clock. I'd always found it can take a good two weeks to really get used to the new time zone. Mr Mac and his class sat on stage and waited patiently to receive their last primary school certificates. Hot chocolates were the promised bounty on our return home. It was getting late and had been a very long and noisy night. An accidental spillage of hot chocolate from Mr Mac's cup onto his sister's arm caused the first explosion that my mother witnessed. As I rushed Miss Lipstick's arm under the tap, Mr Mac fled to his bedroom and descended into a full meltdown. I had envisioned that my children would be saying goodnight to their grandmother wearing crisp white nighties and squealing with delight at her arrival. Instead, we had already gone nuclear. Mr Mac eventually calmed down and apologised. I was embarrassed that the mask of us all coping had prematurely slipped. My mother took it in her stride. She loved him regardless. We all did.

'You've got a *very big* television,' was her next remark to puncture.

'No bigger than a normal television,' I countered. Stop reacting Louise, don't take the bait.

It was as if she was looking at an IMAX screen. I was crushed over these exchanges. I'm not sure what I was looking for, congratulations on giving the children a lovely home, being a good parent? The real question was why did I put so much weight on what she thought? Was I oversensitive? Couldn't I just put Wonder Woman deflection bracelets on? A precarious mother-daughter dynamic began to replay. I could feel myself slowly reverting from adult to sulky teenager.

The night before my operation, Mr Mac had his school formal dance. I was beaming with pride and excitement for him. I dropped him off only after the obligatory hundred photographs had been taken. I returned before the end for the mandatory mother-son dance. It felt such a wonderful last reward for the difficult year that had been. I was so happy that I could share this moment before yet another long stretch of recovery. He, on the other hand, looked like he'd rather poke his own eye out. He had grown up so much over the year. I held him a bit tighter that night.

Thursday 10th December 2015

The next day, it was déjà vu surgery day. I stood at the door to say goodbye to the children before they headed off for the bus. The stage was set, I was ready for my last big performance. A mix of excitement and nerves with an underlying uneasiness of 'Will I wake up again?' I just kept telling myself, 'You got this, you know the drill'. Audrey took me to the surgery and stayed with me until I was wheeled away. I was confident that both Dr Practical and Dr Thorough would work well together and knock it out of the park. I just hoped that my mother and the children would all get along whilst I wasn't there. The children had been so used to just us again, having yet another person in the house and new ways of doing things would be hard for them.

Before I knew it, I was awake and settled into my hospital room wearing surgical stockings and stormtrooper attire on my legs. They gently squeezed my legs to prevent blood flow from slowing down. A large, slow-releasing morphine machine was attached to my arm, releasing its enchantment. I even had my own personal release button. Pain relief, just one click away. It was so incredibly freeing not to be in any pain. I wondered if the nurses were worried that they would need to surgically detach my finger from the button.

I had suggested that my mother take the children to the oval to watch the local Christmas show, followed by fireworks. It was our traditional family outing and a wonderful community event. I didn't want the children to miss out whilst I was in hospital. I knew it would be a wonderful experience of Christmas, Aussie style, for my mother too. The plan was that my mother would extract Mr Mac before the fireworks started as the sound had always been too overbearing for him. There wasn't a massive gap between the end of the show and the start of the fireworks. Everyone was caught off guard. Thankfully, a friend had joined them all just beforehand, pulled his hat down and shielded his ears with her hands. He gazed up in awe at the display. For the first time he stayed until the end. Upon returning home, Mr Mac was quite concerned that my mother hadn't eaten that night and offered to make her some eggs on toast. Perhaps they all fared better when I wasn't there after all. Isn't that always the case?

Relief enveloped me the next day. I savoured the magnitude of this moment. My year bookended by medical interventions was complete. We could all finally move on.

Christmas came early—no cancer in my uterus. That's one less organ to worry about then.

I just wanted to stay in the hospital room, recuperate, and enjoy the room service. It was my own distorted version of a hotel getaway. The moment didn't last long.

My mobile rang.

'You need to come home,' Mr Mac whispered.

It turned out there had been some argy-bargy about toast. He always had four pieces in the four-slotted toaster, all cooked at exactly the same time. My mother proposed more of a Noah's Arc approach—two by two. Her reasoning was sound, this way, it would ensure all four pieces were equally hot. For Mr Mac, this was not reasonable. He promptly threw the two toasted pieces in the bin and put a new four in the toaster. It appeared the change to Mr Mac's breakfast regime was one too many to bear. I would need to leave the hospital early before it became pistols at dawn. My mother never knew he had called. I never knew until recently that he said sorry to her for being rude. Perhaps if I did, I might have stayed in longer.

Wednesday 16th December 2015

The day after coming out of the hospital, it was Mr Mac's final day at school. The Year 6 farewell archway was steeped in tradition. The whole school would line up in two lines across the playground. The school leavers would then weave their way under the arched arms of their peers. It was a symbolic rite of passage from primary school to high school, I didn't want to miss it. I'd only managed to take a few brief walks around the hospital corridors, so I wasn't sure how my legs would fare for this outing. I was determined to be there, even if it meant I would look like a hunched heifer. Thank god for my mother's walking trolley as it gave me something to hold on to. By the time I got into the playground, I was wiped out. The trolley turned into a seat, so I remained seated to watch the activities. Even though most of his friends were going to the same high school as him, Mr Mac was overcome by the significance of this new chapter. It proved to be an emotional day for us all.

The lead up to Christmas felt like Groundhog Day. I had high expectations and lots of frustration at only being able to achieve minimal activity. I regularly needed to lie down. I was also delighted to find myself in the midst of my third and perhaps favourite version of menopause—the surgically induced. It was as if someone had cranked up the heater and we were already in the midst of an Aussie summer. I was hot, sweaty, swollen, and bothered. I would tentatively shuffle around the house. The heavy pressure in my nether regions felt like everything was about to fall out. My umbilical hernia scar made my belly button look like it was smirking at me—at least someone was finding me being indisposed again funny.

Dr Practical had used my original caesarean scar as access. I looked like a magician's assistant who'd been sawn in half and then sewn up like a tightly drawn purse. I had cheekily requested a tummy tuck but was told, in no uncertain terms, that this was general surgery, not plastic surgery. The delightful overhanging flap resting above my scar taunts me to this day. Furthermore, I had hoped that with ovaries, uterus, fallopian tubes, *and* cervix all being removed, I might benefit not only from a washboard stomach, but I would wake up half the size of the woman I was. The histology report shattered those dreams as my entire specimen weighed a measly 46 grams. Even the ovaries were showing 'atrophic' changes, which I believe is the polite way of saying I was a 'shrivelled old lady' now.

Miss Lipstick was curious about the surgery. I took the dignified route and just told her it meant I wouldn't be able to have any more babies.

'Is that because you had your vagina guts out?' She asked innocently.

'Yes … yes, something like that,' I had to turn away to swallow my laughter and hold on to my stitches.

Unfortunately, the Christmas spirit seemed to have skipped our home. A mix of overtired and emotionally spent children home for the holidays and differences in how we did things, meant tensions began to rise. Armageddon was around the corner. Our home had become divided into two camps. I was in the middle.

Less than a week after I'd left the hospital, I was trying to coax Mr Mac away from his PlayStation to come outside. I wanted to capture some sentimental footage of the children on their Christmas bikes. They had been on lay-by and stored in our garage since July. I had envisaged that whilst they were spending Christmas with their father, I could tearfully watch them back on Christmas day. My request proved to be both inconvenient and the final straw for Mr Mac. After all, it would require him to leave a game AND be in the fresh air. It was then that his pent-up fury and frustration tumbled out. His emotions had been safely buried in enamel casing and I'd unwittingly pulled the pin. He raised his foot up and gestured a karate kick towards my stomach. I instinctively recoiled and placed my hand over it for protection. My mother stopped hanging out the washing and came over to intervene. All hell broke loose. Mr Mac screamed at my mother,

'Go back to where you came from Satan.'

Yep. It was the stuff of Christmas movies.

Horrified, I retreated to my bedroom still clutching my stomach. My mother rang their father and asked him to speak to the children to calm them all down. He offered to come and collect them a week early so that I had more time to recover. I was grateful that he did. I needed to rest and recuperate. My cup was now officially empty.

With the children gone, a more relaxed routine befell. We enjoyed puzzles, scrabble and simple activities together. But with this peace and quiet, I became the focus of attention.

'Is that your laugh?' my mother enquired one day. 'I mean is that *really* your laugh?'

I wasn't sure if she was implying that I was putting it on or not.

'I don't remember you *laughing* like that?' she added.

'Would you prefer me *not* to laugh?' I replied indignantly.

Granted, my laugh is a mix of fishwife and witches cackle, but I was just feeling so happy and free that the year was finally coming to a close. I wasn't really prepared to be critiqued for enjoying the moment.

It was at this point, it dawned on me that perhaps I was an object of curiosity to my family. I had spent so many years living abroad that I'd changed from the girl who left their shores. It was natural that it would cause some confusion. Compacted time together and heightened stress, revealed the cracks of my old stories and patterns of behaviour. I had less tolerance for papering over them and not showing up to life fully as my whole self. I needed time for reflection before I could form a different viewpoint of my life.

For years, I'd been like a Labrador yearning for love and attention. I always sought outside validation. The perfectionist trying not to rock the boat, to fit in and satisfy everybody's expectations. I had splintered myself in the process. I didn't blame my family for not recognising me. I didn't even recognise who I was becoming. But, by the end of the year, the rumblings of change were just beginning, and more barriers would come down.

New Year's Eve festivities were quiet and spent at home. I retreated to creature comforts and enjoyed a glass of wine and a packet of crisps. My mother went to bed early. I tucked myself up in bed with a cup of tea. I shed a few tears and stayed awake till midnight. Just to prove to myself that I really had survived the year.

19

Stops and Starts

If the strike of midnight had changed everything for Cinderella, then I was hoping for some of the same. I imagined I would wake up, hair fanned across my pillow, and birds singing around my head. This would be my happily ever after. New year, New you, would be my strapline. I'd surely paid my dues by now, hadn't I? The slate would be wiped clean. I was ready to start my new chapter.

The year turned out to be filled with more stops, than starts.

My mother would soon be flying back home. The children had returned from their father's and the break had provided respite for everyone. My scar was healing, and I was standing more upright. I wanted my parting with my mother to end on a high note, so I organised for a friend to come and stay with the children whilst we enjoyed a last lunch together. The challenge of living so far away is not knowing when I would be seeing her again. I wanted her to leave with the sense that I would be fine, even if I didn't know for sure myself. It was an emotional parting. It was the last of the planned family visits on the horizon. I was back to being alone once more. It would be up to me to make life work again.

Over the coming weeks and months, I lost my mojo. I grappled with the ripple effects of treatment. My body seemingly had the memory of an elephant. The visible patchwork of scars were constant reminders. I felt a complete loss of identity. The daily cancer circus tent had been packed away and I craved its structure. It seemed easier to follow directions than to think for myself. The road ahead was wide open, but I couldn't see a horizon. I may have retaken the proverbial wheel again, but it didn't feel as exhilarating as I'd hoped. My medical appointments gradually began to space out, so did I. I was taking more and more pills to counteract the domino effects of treatment. I wondered if I was beginning to rattle.

I felt an obligation to snap back to 'normal', I just didn't know what that looked like anymore. So many unanswered questions in my head, ranging from the absurd to frankly quite ridiculous. Will I ever be able to have more than two glasses of wine? How long will it take for my hair to grow back properly? Am I always going to look middle-aged? Will this hair ever stop growing back curly? Why has my hair grown back curly on top and straight in my lady garden? Why does this hair keep growing up and wide—will people start to mistake me for a furry sound recorder? Aren't I supposed to be having an 'aha moment' about life? Had I missed something in the small print? Wasn't I supposed to undertake some grand gesture of travelling around the world again? Should I be posting life-affirming statements on social media to inspire the masses? Wasn't I supposed to be having a complete overhaul of my lifestyle? Aren't I supposed to have the wisdom of a guru? Should I be showing up live daily on Instagram in a leotard, body of a 20-year-old, and drinking green juice? Why hadn't my body pinged back quickly? Why were the weighing scales mocking me?

So many damaging questions and highly unrealistic expectations.

Stops and Starts

The mundane elements of life started seeping back in. Everyone settled into their new school year. A wooden trunk arrived packed by my mother with all my old photographs, school yearbooks, historic journals, and memorabilia. The last of my remaining things had now been shipped to Australia, my forever home. It was like unpacking pieces of my childhood and the life that I had not looked at for years. I caught glimpses of the sensitive child I was, who loved being in nature, outside in the woods filled with bluebells, making mud pies, picking flowers, playing with the dogs and cloud watching.

I also found the girl who, after leaving boarding school, worked in a large London department store for several months, so that she could save up to fly to Hong Kong for a Christmas holiday, and stayed a year. In Hong Kong, someone had suggested she model, so she cashed in her last traveller's cheques and booked a studio with an unknown photographer. She managed to blag her way into her first modelling job and flew to Korea for a golfing apparel catalogue. She convinced the photographer that she was an experienced professional model, with her full portfolio in London. The same girl who completed a degree, the first of her family to do so, and worked several jobs to support herself. The girl who became a manager in her early 20s for a global company, moved to the Middle East for a period of time for work and then travelled extensively. Yet here she was now, a shadow of herself. She was at a fork in the road. This adult was both curious of, and grieving that girl in the photos. She was oscillating between who she was and who she was destined to become.

That trunk sent me on a profound journey of self-discovery over the next few years. It was painfully apparent how much more settled I felt when I thought I was dying. I had looked back at my most memorable achievements, children, family, friends, time spent travelling, loving wholeheartedly (often in the wrong places), kicking career goals, and then living a simpler life in the countryside. I had lived a full life with no regrets. I now felt trapped in this fragile and weakened body and fuzzy mind. I wondered if the best of my life was now behind me. I became more anxious as the possibility of a future started to stretch out before me. I was afraid of repeating old stories and patterns. I needed to give myself permission, space and time to heal. But the hits of life just kept on coming.

With every twinge or new symptom, I would fear the worst. My first bone scans showed there was another 'disease' present. Morbid thoughts told me this surely was secondary cancer in my bones. It turned out to be osteoporosis and Paget's disease in my skull. I needed to find some workarounds for these new symptoms. I considered wearing hats again so that if my head grew bigger from Paget's later on, I hadn't missed my window. Ironic, I was just enjoying getting some wind through my hair again.

Lymphedema paid a fleeting visit to my left arm. It took me by surprise as I hadn't had any symptoms the previous year. There is nothing sexier than wearing a cream compression sleeve with fingerless gloves in summer. I had a few visits to a specialist to help release some of the fluid using a pneumatic compression pump to stimulate the flow. The machine was like suction cups on steroids and made the same noise as a breast pump. I was fortunate that my bout was relatively mild compared to others. I can usually tell when I might need additional help as my neck becomes thicker. Unfortunately, polo necks are not suitable for summer.

My first annual mammogram check-in loomed on the calendar. When the day arrived, I took a friend to celebrate with me. After a smooth-sailing mammogram, I sat patiently waiting for the results.

I was reminded of earlier prize-giving days at school. I imagined my name would be called out, and I would be awarded a 'best in treatment' rosette for my efforts. There would be a standing ovation. I would be asked to give a speech.

The lady from the mammogram reappeared in the doorway. I expected her to call her next patient in but instead, she walked over to me,

'Hi, I've just checked the films. We just need to get another film done for your *right* breast.'

Oh no, here we go again.

I felt as though there was a conspiracy between my boobs. Perhaps my right one felt too much attention had been given to the left. Fortunately, the 'shadow' turned out to be a false alarm. I hoped that would be the end of it, but when I walked into the ultrasound, the sonographer was the same lady who'd held my arm tightly the year before. Oh, come on! Not another omen? I'd been told when I was younger that I looked like the actress who played the *Omen*'s mother, but this was getting ridiculous.

It didn't get any better, calcifications were spotted on the ultrasound. I could either take the 'wait and see approach' and a mammogram in six months to see if there were further changes or have a biopsy now. Hello, have you met me? I could hardly wait for two weeks last time. I voted to have a biopsy to rule out anything sinister. The mammographer kindly squeezed me in her lunch hour the next day, just before Easter. I returned home and began comparing these new films with my last set. An irregular game of snap if you will, with a side of google for good measure. The night-time is when my dark thoughts stretch their legs and freely wander. Tonight, would be no different.

This biopsy was unlike the previous ones. I remained seated and upright for this procedure. My boob was clamped down in the machine for over 20 minutes. Everyone circled around, reviewing films and getting my positioning on fleek. The drilling sound was less dental and more digging for gold. I remembered the quietness of the other biopsy needles with fondness. As the machine continued to vibrate, I began to wonder how long my boobs must be. In fact, it was rotating to take samples, not burrowing down. I kept my eyes closed and clenched the bar. My other arm was placed awkwardly for access purposes. The scar was in a state of resistance. There was a sharp burning pain as this tissue pulled further apart. My arm began to shake. Tears rolled down my cheeks. The technicians offered to pause and give me a break, but I gestured for them to continue. I was screaming inside. The final step was to inject a metal fragment to mark the excavation site—a tag and release program. I wondered if I would set airport security alarms off now.

I kept the news of the second biopsy quiet as I had invited friends and their children from Bondi and Bowral for a 'Thank you' party the following week. I didn't want to miss a chance of seeing everyone again. Worst-case scenario, the party becomes my living wake. I directed my attention to getting party decorations, organising food, drinks and clearing the garden. I imagined a playlist with *'I will survive'* and *'All on my own'* whilst singing drunkenly on the karaoke machine 'goodbye' songs to my boobs. The results came in the day before the party. I was given the all-clear. The celebrations would now be even more special. I was the mistress of the microphone that night. Grateful to be able to deliver my heartfelt thanks for everyone's support.

Shortly afterwards, we received notice from the landlord that they were now putting the house on the market. It had been our home and haven for four years. With two dogs and winter upon us, I panicked and rented the first house we saw. It was a much smaller house and would require the dogs to remain outside. I placed an insane pressure on myself to secure a full-time job so that I could buy a house. My misguided reason was that if I got sick again and had to get help with the mortgage, the house could be collateral to repay debts after my death. I didn't want to continue to be a financial burden. I scoured for jobs in the local area. Friends would take me to interviews as I still was not allowed to drive after the operation.

I was going through the motions of life, but my self-esteem was at an all-time low. I still didn't look or feel like myself. I was relieved when I secured a job. I rationalised that this would be our saviour and a solution to saving a deposit. One of the harsh realities of having cancer is that insurance premiums either skyrocket or you can't access them until you have a few more 'cancer-free years' under your belt. This included mortgage insurance. I may have received my get out of free jail card from cancer, but I would remain in limbo land until I reached my five-year clearance. I tied myself in knots and got stuck in the 'we'll be happy when' trap.

The full-time regime was hard for all of us. I wasn't the close at hand mother I had been the previous year. The kids started to act up as if they could only now release their anxiety and angst. It coincided with my appearance on the outside beginning to stabilise. Inside was a different story. I had reverted to spinning multiple plates. The stress of keeping them in the air was taking a gradual toll.

I started to get sick. Really sick. I woke up in the middle of the night, unable to breathe. I sat in the darkness, weighing up my choices. It was 2 am. I finally decided to wake the children and drive to the hospital. Previous experience taught me it was best to go as a group. At the hospital we were taken straight through to the emergency ward. I was surrounded by beeping machines and had an oxygen mask over my face. The children, still in their pyjamas, looked on with apprehension. I tried to look composed to reassure them.

I checked the clock religiously until it was a reasonable time to call. My breathing was shallow as I attempted to speak on the phone to ask a friend for help. ER was full of adult patients calling out in pain. I wanted the children to be extracted as soon as possible. I smiled weakly as they left.

I was admitted and finally taken to my room. I was told that radiotherapy can cause lung damage. My cancer was on my left side, so problems with my heart could also be collateral. The shortness of breath was exasperated with the stress of not knowing if I was able to take another one. I continued gasping for air. I was terrified. A raft of tests was ordered to rule out the usual suspects one by one. The verdict was complex. What had started as laryngitis, had developed into pneumonia secondary pleurisy.

I had taken on too much again, in an attempt to achieve these unrealistic expectations of myself and my life. I failed to listen to the signs from my body before it collapsed again. All this to strive for a future that I now might not even reach. I was petrified that this would be my end and that I hadn't learnt anything. I had to stop pushing my way through life. A combative approach was clearly not the solution. I had strengthened my resilience muscle to the max. I needed to work on *less force* and *more flow*. It was time to put these lessons into practice. I stopped working full time and started working part time. I thought that would give me the balance that

I needed. I would need to learn more about the mind and body connection to really comprehend the concept.

My Christmas 2016 card from Miss Lipstick was a consolation that I was doing some things right, even if I did need to visit the butcher more.

> ***Dear Mum***
> ***Merry Christmas. I know it's been a crazy/ terrible/amazing year for you. But, you always have a smile on your face and a positive attitude. This year should end with a big happy month.***
>
> ***This year was your first year not having breast cancer. Next year should be a nice and freash <fresh> start. This year was quit <quite> busy year for you full of a new job… I also know I have been a bit of trouble included in your crazy things that happened this year.***
>
> ***I think we had like one hunred <hundred> roast chickens, chicken nuggets and chips, baked beans on toast and scrambled eggs so hopefully next year we can bye <buy> more yummy meats from the butchers and now I'm finishing with a poam <poem> made with you on my mind: love Miss Lipstick xxx***
>
> ***When your down you still smile***
> ***When your sad you still think positive***
> ***When you around you make me happy***
> ***Never forget I'll always love you***

The first year after treatment taught me to expect the unexpected. The ensuing years taught me to slow down and let life unfold. A hybrid version of the old and new me continued to show up as life threw more plot twists—three house moves within 18 months, job changes, and unimaginable losses.

Our beautiful Labrador, Coco, suffered kidney failure. She had been the first decision we had made as a family. Coco had been at the heart and centre of everything, providing solace and unconditional love to us all. It was a tragic loss for us to bear, especially so soon after treatment had ended. We had spent many months trying to reverse her condition, but it was time to release her from pain.

We prepared a list of all the things that we would do with her before the time came and slowly ticked them off. I wanted the children to be prepared for the inevitable and for her passing to be peaceful. I'd arranged for the vet to come to our home on a Friday. We needed time to say our goodbyes and a weekend to grieve. For the last couple of hours, I laid on the bed with her and just journaled as she slept. I wanted to capture those precious last moments. As the time grew closer for the vet to arrive, I set the scene with candles and soothing background music. I wanted it to be picture perfect and serene.

However, death, just as in life, cannot be tightly controlled. Coco reacted to the medication and fought so much her adrenaline spiked, she started foaming at the mouth. As the children said their goodbyes, I held her head in my hands to prevent them from seeing her eyes roll to the back of her head. It was horrific from start to finish. I stayed with her till her last breath. She had been with me during my darkest hours.

After her body was taken away, I was physically sick. I called the children and told them to change into their PJs and come into my bedroom. It was 5.30 pm. I took out my iPad and told them that we would look through photos of her together and share our favourite stories. I even read a bit from the journaling I had completed earlier. I wanted them to remember her in her prime, and for all that she had given us. I'd never grieved like that before. It was the first time our family released our collective emotions and processed our grief together. It took a long time to erase those last moments from our minds.

My mental health had started to deteriorate. Introspection was not always my friend. I was losing my spark of hope, only enjoying fleeting moments of feeling empowered. I felt I was somehow failing at life. Why did it seem so much easier for others? I felt guilty for not finding pleasure in every minute of every day, especially with this precious second chance at life. I sought the traditional methods of help, medication, talking therapies and support groups, but they only scratched the surface. They provided band-aid solutions to keep me going, but the slow rise of discontent kept rumbling on. I was still afraid of showing up as my true authentic self.

I attended a local residential wellbeing program for a week. It opened my eyes to the power of past conditioning and limiting beliefs. It was like finding a key to how the unseen has so much impact on our behaviours and body. I hadn't realised there was such a significant connection between the mind and body and the clues they provide for uncovering the root causes of unhappiness. It was uncomfortable and hard work. To be honest, I'd imagined more of a quick fix and lying around with cucumbers on my eyes. I left with more questions, but it ignited a hunger inside to delve deeper into this work. Life continued. I tried to find a balance between work, study, and life. In reality, I was still firefighting problems and still couldn't quite see the bigger picture.

A short time after our loss of Coco, my father's health deteriorated. Friends rallied so that I could fly over to England. I brought forward my annual testing so that I could ensure that I wouldn't risk any complications. I drove straight from the airport to be with him. It was the first time I had seen him in four years. He had been diagnosed with cancer the year before my diagnosis and was now suffering from secondary cancer. It was confronting to see him this way, but I will be forever grateful to have been by his side for those last few hours. Something profound happened with this experience. My fear of death dissipated, and an awakening began.

I extended my trip to be able to stay for the funeral. Time differences meant juggling arrangements for the children in the night-time and helping prepare for the funeral during the day. It was a tempestuous time.

'We just need to get through this day, and then we can go to our own countries to grieve,' my sister announced the day of the funeral.

That was the pivotal moment that I recognised I had been holding my emotions back to suit others. The feelings genie was now out of the bottle. I realised it was not for me to change how people saw me; it was for me to be my own change.

I returned home and grief became my master. I grieved my father, my old life, and the old me. I could not sleep at night, focus or complete even the simplest of projects. It was as if I lived on a separate timeline from everyone else. I remember taking some time out to meet a friend for a pedicure. She was a bit late for the appointment, so they had already filled the basin with warm water to soak my feet in. I was enjoying this small token of pampering when the technician pulled the plug to empty the basin. He had forgotten to secure the other outlet and the water cascaded to the floor. My leather boots were on the floor beside me and were promptly doused in water. It was an accident. They would be dry in no time, but I was beside myself. They were leather military-style boots that I had worn for my father's funeral, a nod to his naval background and I had thought they would be a comforting reminder when I returned home. Seeing them now spoilt, felt like I had somehow discarded his memory. It triggered a surge of pent-up emotions to be released. I texted my friend to forewarn her that I was on the precipice of a breakdown. I feared if I used spoken words, I would unleash a tsunami of grief. All I could think of was retreating home to a safe space.

After the nail salon incident, I kept out of sight. Months passed, and I still had no control of my escaping emotions. I cried at a job interview when I mentioned his name. I held my breath watching the royal wedding when one of the hymns from the funeral was sung. It was as if all my senses were on high alert and at a constant tipping point. The walnut shell covering my heart had been cracked and everything was oozing out. I began to further peel back the layers of old conditioning. I looked back with gratitude at all of my major milestones. These events revealed life lessons that became stepping stones to the person I am today.

My emotions were now a faucet that couldn't be shut off. It was finally time to fully reconnect to myself, explore, heal and grow. The balance I was seeking was not outside of myself; it was the wisdom within. It would require a holistic approach to my healing. I started to study a range of holistic tools and healing practices.

I attended workshops, live events, and learnt from many mentors about energy, emotions, mind and body. Sorting through what resonated and discarding what didn't. I started to surrender to the process and shift from the grief of what had been lost towards gratitude for what I had gained.

My eyes began to open to new opportunities and a new way of living my life. I started creating building blocks towards my future dreams. I may not have had all the pieces, but the puzzle was slowly coming together.

20

Five Years Later

'Louise.'

I followed Dr Thorough down the corridor and into his office where I'd been so many times before. As he closed the door, he turned around and shouted, 'Congratulations on your five-year clearance!' His hands were raised triumphantly, and he was smiling exuberantly at me.

'Thank you,' I replied quietly.

His arms dropped down, and he looked a little deflated. I was officially the party pooper.

'It's just that I saw the oncologist the other day and he said there isn't a certificate or letter when you reach five years?' I sounded like a four-year-old.

He looked perplexed.

'It's just that when I used to work at a cancer organisation years ago, we were told that when you reached five years, you were called a "survivor". I thought we'd be given a record to give to insurance companies,' I said sheepishly, trying to explain myself.

To be fair, it was only on my mind as I was about to go abroad and thought it could be used as 'proof of life' for my travel insurance premium.

'Louise, there is no letter. You just tell the travel insurance the date of your operation and that you have been clear since then.'

'Oh,' I responded, feeling a little churlish for having asked.

'As you brought this up, I just need to explain why there is no letter. Breast cancer and skin cancer are two cancers that we can't officially say are ever 'cured'. All I can tell you is that some of my patients were not as fortunate as you to still be here, he explained gently.

'Because it's now been five years, today will be your final examination. I will no longer be seeing you from this point forward. Unless of course, something is detected at your annual checks or in-between' he added.

I shuffled my way to the examination bed at the side of the room to undress. As I took off my bra, a distinct sound of something hard dropping on the floor reverberated around the room.

'What was that?' Dr Thorough asked.

'What?'

'That sound of something dropping.'

Five Years Later

'Ummm ...' Stall for time again. Stall for time ... how do I explain this without him thinking I'm weird? I grabbed my shirt to provide some modesty. Better to be weird and covered than just weird.

'Umm, it was a crystal, it fell out from my bra,' I added, trying to sound all 'nothing to see here' and laughed nervously.

'A crystal?' his eyes widened.

'Yes, a small raw ruby stone. It fits in where the dent in my breast is.' Of course, mention that too Louise, it will make much more sense now.

Thankfully, he just asked what it looked like. We both started looking at the floor around the examination table.

'Is that it there?' I squealed.

'No, that's not it, it's just a fly.'

'Oh, I've found it, I've found it,' I repeatedly shouted as if I'd just won the lottery. I excitedly pointed to a small stone jammed between the bed and the wall.

'We just need a hanger to get it out,' I added.

'I don't have a hanger,' he replied.

'There's one,' I excitedly pointed to the back of the door.

'Yes, but it's got my jacket on.'

He could tell that I would be unlikely to let this go and reluctantly took his jacket off the hanger. Rather than handing it to me, he graciously crouched down on the floor, in his suit trousers. He yanked the hanger up and down a couple of times to loosen the grip.

'I've never seen or done anything like this before,' he laughed and handed me the ruby.

> My mission in life is not merely to *survive*, but to *thrive*; & to do so with some *passion*, some compassion, some *humour*, and some style.

MAYA ANGELOU

Afterword

I thought that my cancer diagnosis was to be the full stop to my life. It turned out to be a C-stop amongst an array of life's curveballs. The gift that cancer has given me is that it has opened my eyes to possibilities and jolted me into action. It broke me down so that I had no choice but to build myself back up even stronger. It prompted me to think about what type of life I'd want to live if I only had a few years left and to lose attachment to the old stories I had told myself.

I realised it was not too late to take charge of my life and rewrite my storyline. I'd spent much of my life 'people-pleasing' and seeking outside validation before understanding that you will not always be everyone's cup of tea. I had kept busy to distract myself from facing the root causes of my own unhappiness. I'd let stress build up in my body by stifling my emotions to the point that my body ultimately broke down. I would need to create a new relationship with my body and thank it for its reliance and fortitude. To embrace my scars as the roadmap of my life experiences and what I had overcome. My body is really the unsung hero of my story. It has given my children life and a new one to me. I now listen to the whispers of my body and the intuitive messages it provides.

I learnt that my wisdom was held within. To be guided by life's challenges for the lessons they provided. To allow my raw emotional mess and vulnerability to be revealed and to sit with the triggers of discomfort that might result. I worked hard to find alternatives to my conditioned approach of distract, suppress or shutdown. For if I couldn't feel difficult emotions and accept both sides of myself, then how could I ever fully enjoy life? I take little steps each day and try to be gentle with myself when I falter.

We are all products of how we were raised, the mistakes we make and the stories we have held since childhood. This is what makes us human and the people we are today. But we have a choice of how we move forward. Understanding my past helped me heal and grow. I am responsible for creating my own happiness, regardless of my circumstances. I am grateful to the many family, friends and people who have come into my life during this time, before and after. It is not easy to see your loved ones in pain and struggling. I love and respect them for being there for me.

We have endured some unprecedented events since I started writing this book from bushfires and floods in Australia, to a worldwide pandemic, COVID-19. The silver lining has been a shift in the dynamic with my own family through regular WhatsApp calls where we have shared our ups and downs, much laughter and become closer. It is a timely reminder of the power of connection and being open-hearted to everyone's outlook on life. I am also happy to report that Mr Mac no longer refers to his much-loved grandmother as Satan.

I continue to practise balancing and protecting my energy. I have a deeper respect for the mind and body connection. I discovered I didn't need to be rescued; I could rescue myself. I am more interested in showing both sides of my human experience than before. I am learning to be less reactive to life, have firmer boundaries and

Afterword

work with the flow of life. I remain a work in progress. I am so grateful to be living a more full and vibrant life now. One that is more authentically aligned to my values. Whatever your full stop moment has been, my wish is that you too will rise stronger—and collectively, we enjoy a brighter future together.

There are no full stops in life, but there is power in the pause. The only guaranteed full stop in life is death. The worst way to live is when you aren't living as your authentic self. Life is for living and for taking risks. You are the creator of your own happiness and for living a life with no full stops. What's stopping you?

❝ Time is too slow for those who wait,
too swift for those who fear,
too long for those who grieve,
too short for those who rejoice,
but for those who love,
time is eternity. ❞

HENRY VAN DYKE

Acknowledgements

They say it takes a village to raise a child. Writing this book took that concept to a whole other level. A cross-continent approach of asking friends, family and colleagues to read anywhere from a sentence to a chapter, to the whole book. I thank you all for your patience, guidance, hand-holding, listening ears and encouragement. I could never have imagined at the start of this process how deeply profound, challenging, thought-provoking, enlightening and healing it would be. From releasing old stories that I had held on to for many years, to finding new meaning within the madness of this life-changing event. I am truly grateful for all the heart-led people I surround myself with today.

There are some particular people I would like to highlight who went above and beyond to ensure that this book was completed: Suzie, Michelle and Viv for reading my initial drafts when I could barely get my fingers to engage with the keyboard. Lucy P for lovingly receiving my first draft when I was in a tailspin. She advised me that I had scribed two books (I like to think of that as over-delivering—others would say that was just throwing words down on paper with no clear direction!). And Kirstine, for helping me see the wood for the trees.

Thank you Jo, for encouraging me to write a long time ago and for introducing me to the wonderful Karin. Thank you, Karin, for your gentle guidance and shining a light on the parts that needed to be explored further. To my fellow authors from the August retreat 2019, especially Dr Bec and Azita and the editors and team at the publishers; thank you for always making me feel part of a group huddle and cheering me on, even as I stumbled towards the last full stop.

There are so many people who supported us throughout my cancer journey, I fear it would read like the end credits of a movie if I listed you all. I know and remember each and every one and the part you played in holding our family together. I hope you know I would be there for you in a heartbeat, so please don't hesitate to ask.

A most sincere and heartfelt thanks to the medical team of doctors, nurses, volunteers and people behind the scenes for giving me this second chance. I'd also like to acknowledge the following charities for the vital services and respite you provided: The McGrath Foundation, Breast Cancer Network Australia, Can Assist, PAWS Pet Therapy dogs and handlers, Look Good Feel Better, Highlands Sisterhood Dinner Drive, The Cancer Council, The OTIS Foundation, YWCA Encore and Quest for Life Foundation.

To my family overseas a massive thank you. I wouldn't be who or where I am today without your love and moral support. To my mother, thank you for instilling in me the ability to be strong-willed, determined and to never give up. To my late father, thank you for your humour and for encouraging me to be ever curious and a lifelong learner. To my sisters, for being my wing women at times of crisis. I am anticipating smoother waters ahead. To my Uncle M, for being a steady port, especially during that year and to Trudie, for providing a safe haven and listening ear. I love you all.

Acknowledgements

My intention has always been to share my story from my perspective, how I felt at the time and what I learnt as a result. I continue to evolve and grow. I hope to forever remain curious about life and learning and to find something new to laugh about every day.

Finally, to my children, you have taught me so much about myself and what I am capable of. I hope you feel my love for you always, even when you don't put things in the dishwasher. I love you both and I am so very proud of you.

> I am not what happened to me, I am what I choose to become.
>
> **CARL JUNG**

About the Author

Louise was born on the Rock of Gibraltar in 1971, the youngest of three daughters to parents Lieutenant Commander Roger S James RN (Rtd) and Annette James, a Senior Registered Nurse.

Louise spent her formative years in Bath, England. She was a sensitive child with an overactive imagination who spent hours cloud watching, dreaming and drawing before announcing she wanted to be a writer at the tender age of nine.

She has been fortunate enough to enjoy a rich tapestry of life experiences and other cultures through her work and travels from Europe, USA, Middle East, Hong Kong, South America, South Africa, Asia and beyond. She enjoyed a successful career as a strategic marketing and business development professional working with some of the most recognisable and global brands in the corporate and not-for-profit sector. She has called Australia home since 2001.

Following her brush with breast cancer in 2015, she decided to take a more holistic approach to life and completed a diploma in Holistic Counselling and other healing modalities. Louise merges her wealth of life experiences and business acumen to provide holistic guidance for her clients, both personally and professionally. She empowers women to reconnect to their inner wisdom and healing capacity so they can create a balanced and successful life on their terms.

Louise's life-long love of writing led her to publish her first book *No Full Stops* with the vision that by sharing our stories, we can help others **connect**, **heal** and **grow**. Louise is an inspirational, authentic and engaging storyteller and speaker, and shares her diverse stories of resilience and self-care.

She is a mother to two extraordinary teenagers, a middle-aged Labrador (Daisy) and a new puppy (Buddy). They all live together in the beautiful Southern Highlands, south of Sydney. Louise can be found in the garden, cloud watching, taking photos, laughing at her own jokes and drinking copious cups of tea. Louise still continues to look for signs from the universe, much to the eye-rolling of her children.

For more information, please visit her website: Louisejames.com

You can connect with Louise on:

Instagram @louisejames888
Facebook @louisejames888
LinkedIn @louisejames888

Reflections

Reflections

Reflections

www.ingramcontent.com/pod-product-compliance
Lightning Source LLC
Chambersburg PA
CBHW072050110526
44590CB00018B/3113